Oeconomicus

Xenophon Xenophon, Bernard John Hayes

Prospectus of Classes

FOR THE

EXAMINATIONS

OF THE

UNIVERSITY OF LONDON.

All communications should be addressed—

THE PRINCIPAL,

University Correspondence College,

Cambridge.

University Correspondence College.

RECENT SUCCESSES.

At both **MATRICULATION** Exams., 1887, EVERY Pupil who went up was successful.

At **INTER. ARTS**, 1887, twenty pupils passed (only three of whom were in the Second Class), a result greater than that of any other College or Classes.

A copy of the Pass List will be sent free on application to any intending correspondent.

In the Honours Examination, Second and Third Class Honours were obtained at Inter. Arts, and First, Second, and Third Class Honours at **INTER. SCIENCE** by our students.

At **B.A.**, 1887, ten Pupils passed, out of twelve who went up.

In Jan. 1888, four students took Honours at Matric., one qualified for University Prize.

At Prelim. Sci. one-fourth of the whole list of those who passed the entire examination were U.C.C. students.

These successes do not include those in Oral Classes or by individual Tutors, one of whom alone passed twenty-seven at B.A. during 1886 and 1887.

ABSENCE OF FAILURES.

The record is still unbroken that
NO STUDENT
of University Correspondence College
EVER FAILED
at an Examination for which he had worked fully through the Ordinary Course.

PRIZES.

A Prize of *Two Guineas* is awarded on the result of *each* Matriculation Examination to the

PRIVATE STUDENT

who takes the highest place at the Examination.

AT EACH JUNE EXAMINATION.

The Two Guinea Prize will be awarded, and also

A STUDENTSHIP
OF
TEN AND A HALF GUINEAS.

If the winner heads the Matriculation List, an additional Prize of

TEN GUINEAS

will be given. The two latter are open only to Students of University Correspondence College, the former to all private students who send [illegible] list

CONTENTS.

Prospectus of Books by the Tutors for London University Examinations may be had, post-free, on application.

University Correspondence College.

MATRICULATION EXAMINATION.

(*In 1887, every pupil who went up passed, at Jan '88, Four took Honours, one obtaining marks qualifying for University Prize*)

The *General Method of Work* (see p. 4) is employed in preparation for this Examination, the special Authors, etc. for the half-year being carefully gone over and additional Test Papers on them provided.

Students are not admitted to the Systematic Courses unless they possess—

In Languages—a knowledge of Accidence, up to and including the Regular Verb; in Mathematics—Euclid, Books I and II., Algebra, First Four Rules, Arithmetic, a fair all-round knowledge; in English—a good grounding.

There are two Courses open to qualified students:

I. The Ordinary Course.

(*All fees are strictly inclusive, and payable as arranged on joining*)

	£.	s.	d.
Any single Subject	1	11	6
Composition Fee for *all* Subjects	6	6	0

An Ordinary Course consists of eighteen lessons (or sets of lessons) in each subject, in addition to Author Papers. If all subjects are being taken, it is generally best to study half one week and the remainder the next, distributing the work over about a year, reckoning vacations

As the number of Matriculation students is now so large, a class is started on the first Saturdays in February, March, April, May, June, and July, and the last in August, September, October, November, and December. Intending students should join a fortnight before the date of commencement.

For the benefit of those who have failed in one Examination, and wish to proceed to the next, or for those who can devote all their time to study, there is

II. A Special Course,

beginning eighteen weeks before each Examination.

No one should join this course, however, who has any new subject to learn from the beginning—except, perhaps, Mechanics, or Experimental Science, in which case his other work should be good all round, and Mathematics especially strong. Students joining late receive the full number of papers.

	£.	s.	d.
One Subject	1	11	6
For each additional Subject	1	1	0
Composition Fee (for *all* Subjects)	5	15	6

For Self-Preparation Courses, see page 10 of Prospectus.

PRELIMINARY COURSES

for those not qualified to commence the Ordinary Course are arranged according to the pupil's requirements, at the rate of One Guinea for Twelve Lessons. Composition Fee for two or more.

INTERMEDIATE ARTS EXAMINATION.

Ordinary Course.

Before beginning the Ordinary Course in any subject for Intermediate Arts, the student is assumed to possess a knowledge of it up to Matriculation standard. As Greek and French are alternative at Matriculation, Special Preliminary Courses have been arranged for these (see p. 7). A new class is formed on the first Saturdays of September, October, November, and December. Those joining early have the special advantage of frequent short revisions.

FEES.

(Strictly inclusive, and payable as arranged on joining.)

	£	s.	d.
Mathematics * or Latin	2	12	6
Greek, English,† or French...	2	2	0
Composition fee at a reduction for two or more subjects.			
All Subjects for Intermediate Arts Pass	9	9	0

A single Pass Course consists of not less than thirty Lessons. The advantage of this over shorter courses is obvious. The pupil sustains an interest in his work more readily, and gains confidence from the knowledge that the proper amount of attention is being given to each part, and that all will be gone over and recapitulated in good time for the Examination.

Two Years' Course for Inter. Arts.

Although we do not recommend the average student to take two years in preparation for Inter. Arts, still there are some students whose time is so very limited that it is impossible to prepare in one year. We have, therefore, made arrangements for students to distribute their work over more than a year. We prefer them to begin the third week in either October, February, or May. As they require the use of a set of Papers for two years, instead of for one, as is usually the case, and as the postages are heavier, the fee is increased by half-a-guinea in all subjects for each extra term of preparation.

In case a student finds it impossible from illness or other cause to go up for the Examination he intended, favourable arrangements are made for redistribution of his lessons.

---

* No effort has been spared to make the Mathematics Course a success; it is carefully graduated, and smoothes the difficulties of the subject; a type of every Examination question is solved, and in Conics an Illustrative Example is introduced after nearly every paragraph in the text-book. The Full Course consists of thirty Lessons in Trigonometry, thirty in Algebra, thirty in Geometry, twenty in Conics, ten in Arithmetic, and each Lesson is followed by a set of questions.

† A full translation of the Early English extracts is provided.

INTERMEDIATE ARTS EXAMINATION.

Special Courses.

For the sake of students who are unable to join early, as well as for Matriculation Honoursmen, Special Courses, which consist of the same lessons as the Ordinary Courses without Revision Lessons, are commenced in the second week of February.

	£	s.	d.
Mathematics or Latin	2	2	0
Greek, English,* or French	1	11	6
Composition fee at a reduction for three or more.			
All Subjects	7	7	0

Short Courses,

Consisting of about twelve Lessons, and completely covering the ground required in — (1) Analytical Geometry, (2) Latin Grammar, (3) Roman History, (4) Latin Authors, (5) Greek Grammar, (6) Greek Authors, (7) French, (8) Early English*, (9) Latin Prose, are worked from the first Saturday in April or, by special arrangement, any time before the Exam , at a fee of one guinea each, three subjects £2. 12s. 6d These Special Courses are intended (1) for those who do not wish to have complete preparation in all the branches of a subject, (2) for those who cannot join till late, (3) to serve as a Recapitulation. With the exception of Latin Prose, they are included in the Special and Ordinary Courses. Students wishing to join for them before the time stated, may in some cases do so.

Preliminary Courses in Greek and French·

As *both* these subjects are required at Inter. Arts, and only one at Matriculation, special arrangements have been made for Inter. Arts students to take them from the beginning where necessary.

January Matriculants should start the course as soon as convenient after the result is announced, though special arrangements can be made for each applicant. June Matriculants may begin early in July, or on the second Saturday in August, by working during the Vacation, and by taking the later lessons two a week they may complete the Preliminary Course in good time for the Ordinary Inter. Arts Course of the same year.

Candidates who wish to go up for Inter. Arts in the year following their Matriculation can be fully prepared to begin the Inter Arts Course in either Greek or French by means of a month's residence at Burlington House, Cambridge (*see page* 15)

Self-Preparation Courses.

The Ordinary, Special, and Short Courses for Inter. Arts may be taken by *Self-Preparation* for particulars, *see page* 10.

Honours Courses.

(*See page* 11.)

* A full translation of the Early English extracts is provided.

University Correspondence College.

BACHELOR OF ARTS EXAMINATION.

(*In 1887—First Session of Preparation for B.A.—Ten out of Twelve passed.*)

The General Method of Work is pursued for this Examination, Special Papers for the prescribed Authors and Special Periods being provided. The Test Papers are compiled exclusively from questions set at previous Examinations, except when the present regulations have not been sufficiently long in force to admit of this, or when solutions are easily obtainable (*e.g.*, from our "B.A. Mathematics"). In such cases questions *of the same type* have been introduced.

Ordinary Course.—An Ordinary Course in any subject embraces Thirty Lessons. In Latin and Greek each of these consists of two parts: the first part covering the Grammar and General History; the second thirty papers comprising two kinds, *A* and *B*—the *A* papers prepare for the Unseens (now one of the most difficult and important subjects at B.A.), and in Latin, also for Prose, the *B* papers take up the Authors and Special Periods. There is a great advantage in detailed courses like these, with full Notes and Hints to every lesson, over a series of Test Papers whose main purpose is to correct a student's errors rather than show him in advance how to avoid them:—by help of the easy graduation a greater interest is sustained in the work, the specialities of the Examinatien are brought out in stronger relief, time is economised, and confidence gained from the knowledge that the proper amount of attention is being given to each part, and progress more surely counted.

	£.	s.	d.
FEES.—Full Preparation for the Examination ...	12	12	0
Any single Subject	3	13	6
Additional for second and third Subjects, each	3	3	0

The best time to commence the Ordinary Course is at the beginning of the September in the year in which Inter. Arts has been passed; but, as this is inconvenient for many students, there are classes commencing in the first weeks of October, November, and December; arrangements can also be made to suit each applicant.

The lessons are distributed over the whole session from the time of joining, short recesses being provided for revision. Students joining late are worked through the vacations if they desire it.

Special Course.—In this Course, the Lessons and Author Papers are the same as in the Ordinary Course, but the Revision Papers are omitted, the number being thus reduced to twenty-four. It is, therefore, specially convenient for those who have previously failed at the Examination, or who are unable to begin early in the session; the former should, if possible, commence within a week of the publication of the Pass List. Classes also begin in the third week of February, March, and April; arrangements can also be made for individual cases as in the Ordinary Course.

	£.	s.	d.
FEES.—Full Preparation for the Examination ..	10	10	0
Any single Subject	3	3	0
Additional for second and third Subjects, each	2	12	6

For **Self-Preparation Courses**, see page 10.

University Correspondence College.

BACHELOR OF ARTS EXAMINATION.

The **Two Years' Course** is designed for those students whose time is so limited that it is impossible to prepare in one year, but we would here warn candidates for the degree that to rust between Inter. Arts and B.A. is most dangerous; eighteen months' study preceded by a rest of six months is no better than a year's continuous work. The following plan of study is recommended to the ordinary student who cannot give an average of four hours a day for fifty weeks.—

First Year.—College Work in Classics (Ordinary Papers) and Mathematics, or Mental and Moral Science, omitting the revision lessons. Private reading of some of the English, or study of French, not omitting frequent translation. Any spare time may be profitably spent in a preliminary reading of the Classical Authors prescribed; or, as a help in Unseen work, in reading over a book other than that set for the Exam., but by the same Author.

Second Year.—College work in Classics, *A* and *B* papers, Revision lessons in Classics (Ordinary), English or French and Mathematics, or Mental and Moral Science; private recapitulation of first year's work before taking the College Revision Lessons.

Short Courses in Special Subjects, consisting of from twelve to fourteen lessons, and completely covering the ground required, are provided in—

	£.	s.	d.
(i.) Latin Grammar and Composition	1	11	6
(ii.) Latin Composition and Unseens	1	11	6
[Unseens may be taken along with (i.) for an additional fee of 10s. 6d.]			
(iii.) Roman History, including Special Period, and Geography	1	11	6
(iv.) Latin Authors and Special Period of History ...	1	11	6
[The Authors may be taken along with (i.), (ii.), or (iii.) for an additional fee of 10s 6d.]			
(v.) Greek Grammar and Unseens	1	11	6
(vi.) Extended Course of Greek Unseens	1	11	6
[Course (v.) may be taken to include (vi.) by payment of an additional fee of 10s. 6d.]			
(vii.) Grecian History, including Special Period, and Geography . ..	1	11	6
(viii.) Greek Authors and Special Period of History ...	1	11	6
[Greek Authors may be taken along with (vii.) for an additional fee of 10s. 6d.]			
(ix.) Logic *or* (x.) Psychology and Ethics ...	1	11	6
(xi.) French	2	2	0
(xii.) Extended Course in Latin Prose	1	11	6

It is probable that before Easter, 1889, Short Courses may be arranged in

(xiii.) Mechanics *or* (xiv.) Astronomy	1	11	6

and in some of the branches of Pure Mathematics.

A favourable composition fee is charged when several short Courses are taken, especially if in kindred subjects. With slight exception, these Short Courses may be taken up any time after Christmas.

SELF-PREPARATION COURSES.
For Matriculation, Inter. Arts, and B.A.

Students who do not wish to go to the expense of being fully prepared, but who wish to know the scope of the Examination, the principal points to be attended to, and to regulate their reading and economize time, may take

Self-Preparation Courses.

If, in addition, full preparation be required in weak subjects, a favourable composition fee will be charged

For Self-Preparation, weekly lessons are given, each consisting of a scheme for study, selections from text-books, distinction of important points, hints, notes on difficult and salient portions, etc , and illustrative examples with selected text-book exercises in Mathematics. At the end of the week a Test Paper (compiled from previous Examination Papers in fixed subjects) for self-examination is provided, and followed by complete solutions to it *The* differences between these and other courses are, that students' answers have *not* to be sent to the tutor, and special arrangements have to be made as to solution of difficulties. The lessons are sent out on the same dates as in the Ordinary and Special Courses; or by arrangement at any time up to the month before the Exam , so proving useful for revision.

Fees for Self-Preparation Courses.

(*Postages, as in other Classes, included*)

MATRICULATION.

	£.	s.	d.
Two Subjects			
If extending over not more than six months ...	1	1	0
,, ,, more than six months ..	1	11	6
Additional for each Subject	0	10	6
Composition Fee for all Subjects			
If extending over not more than six months ...	2	2	0
,, ,, more than six months ..	3	3	0

INTER. ARTS.

Any single Subject	1	1	0
Three Subjects	2	12	6
Composition Fee for all Subjects	4	4	0

BACHELOR OF ARTS.

Single Subjects	1	11	6
Composition Fee for all Subjects	5	5	0

For other Examinations there are no Self-Preparation Courses except in Mathematics Pure and Mixed.

HONOURS EXAMINATIONS.

Inter. Arts Honours.

In *Mathematics* and *Latin* the Honours Courses consist of thirty Lessons, to each of which, as the requirements are so wide, there are several parts, to render the step to B.A. Honours as gentle as possible, these Courses have been made very full, and the greatest care betowed upon them.

Fee for each Course .. ... £6. 6s.

Students are allowed to take two years over the Honours Courses in Mathematics and Latin without extra fee

In French either fifteen or thirty Lessons may be taken.

	£.	s.	d
Fee for the shorter Course (30 Papers)	3	3	0
For the longer Course (45 Papers)	4	14	6

In Mathematics a student cannot profitably enter upon the Honours Course without a previous knowledge equal to that required for the B.A Pass Pure Examination. In Latin and French a knowledge of the Inter. Arts Pass requirements is necessary.

In English there are fifteen Lessons over and above the Pass Course. As we wish to encourage our students to take up this Course (which may be commenced at any time up to February), the fee for the present will be only £1. 11s 6d.; and a Money Prize of £5 will be given to that student who takes highest Honours, if not less than six join. In view of the new Honours in English at B.A this should become a favourite course.

B.A. Honours Examination.

For B A. Honours the remarks at the top of the page headed "M A. Examination" apply; one, two, or three years being necessary according to a student's knowledge on joining

Mathematics.—For those who have only done up to Inter. Arts Pass standard, 90 lessons would be required, spread over about three years. Fee £15 15s.

Assuming a knowledge of B A. Pass subjects, two years might suffice for the 60 lessons (several parts to each). Fee £11. 11s

Students who took Honours at Inter. Arts, not below the Second Class, 30 lessons. Fee £6. 6s

Students not falling in any of these three classes will be treated according to the number of lessons required

Mental and Moral Science—45 lessons (not including the Pass Course). Fee £9. 9s.

English.—45 lessons (including the Pass Course). Fee £6 6s.

Classics.—The full course preparing for B.A. Honours consists of 60 lessons. Fee £11. 11s. Students who have taken Honours in Latin at Inter. Arts may dispense with some or all of the Latin Papers according to their proficiency on joining. In such cases a proportionate fee will be charged.

Particulars of Honours Courses for other Examinations on application.

University Correspondence College.

MASTER OF ARTS EXAMINATION.

Systematic preparation is offered for this Examination by tutors of the highest standing, several of whom took the Highest Honours attainable at London in their branches. In general, the course is spread over two or three years, corresponding to the stages mentioned below, but, with the exception of the Notes, Papers, and Hints, which apply equally to all going up for the same Examination, the tuition is purely individual, and lessons can be taken exactly at the student's convenience. Each course consists of at least 30 lessons. Parts of the Courses may be taken at proportionate fees

In Mathematics there are three stages to be taken by a student who has acquired only a knowledge of B.A. Pass subjects—

	£	s.	d.
First Stage, equivalent to the Inter. Arts Honours Course, assuming only the B A. Pass Course, which it however recapitulates. Fee	6	6	0
Second Stage, requiring Knowledge of First Stage, and leading up to B.A Honours standard, and recapitulating previous work Fee	6	6	0
Composition Fee for Stages I. and II.	11	11	0
Third Stage, being the additional subjects required for M.A., and revision of previous stages. Fee ...	10	10	0
Composition Fee for the Three Stages	21	0	0
In Mental and Moral Science.			
First Stage, B A. Honours subjects, excluding the special authors. Fee	6	6	0
Second Stage, assuming B.A. Honours standard, and preparing for M.A. Fee...	10	10	0
Classics.			
First Stage, Inter. Arts Honours. Fee ...	6	6	0
Second Stage, B.A. Honours Fee	6	6	0
Composition Fee for Stages I. and II	11	11	0
Third Stage, preparing for M A , and assuming an attainment of B A. Honours work. Fee ..	10	10	0
Composition Fee for the Three Stages	21	0	0
Languages in Branch IV.			
First Stage, equivalent to B.A. Honours	11	11	0
Second Stage, assuming a knowledge of the work of First Stage	10	10	0
Composition Fee for both Stages	21	0	0

INTER. SCIENCE AND PRELIM. SCIENTIFIC.

(In July, 1887, First, Second, and Third Class Honours were obtained.)

The *General Method of Work* is here supplemented by drawings, salts for analysis, and other practical aids.

	£.	s.	d.
(1) **Pure Mathematics.**—See page 6, under Intermediate Arts			
(2) **Mixed Mathematics.**—Fifteen Lessons, according to "General Method of Work"... ... ... Fee	1	11	6
Self-Preparation Course	1	1	0
(3) **Chemistry.**—Thirty Lessons, on the usual plan in Theoretical Chemistry, and salts for analysis sent Fee	3	3	0
(4) **Physics.**—The Course consists of 30 double lessons, two subjects being taken simultaneously ... Fee	3	3	0
(5) **Biology.**—In this subject full directions for work are given, and numerous sketches provided			
Fee for the Course of 30 Lessons	3	3	0
Additional for direction of Practical Work	1	1	0

Intending correspondents are warned that it is next to impossible to begin this subject without practical assistance, and cannot be admitted to the classes without the tutor thinks they have a fair prospect of success.

Full preparation for Inter. Science	12	12	0
,, ,, Preliminary Science	10	10	0

Honours Fees on application.

Private tuition and Laboratory Practice for these Examinations, as well as for **Inter. M.B.**, may be obtained in London at any time during the year.

B.Sc. EXAMINATION.

According to the *General Method of Work*—

Any single Subject	5	5	0
Full Preparation for the Examination, excluding practical work	12	12	0

Honours Fees on application.

Private tuition and Laboratory practice in London by arrangement

LL.B. EXAMINATIONS.

Students are prepared for these Examinations on a special system, under the direction of a London LL.B., Double Honours, First in First Class.

Full preparation for the Pass, Intermediate or Final LL.B., 60 Lessons	12	12	0

Single Subjects at proportionate rates.

Honours Fees on application.

University Correspondence College.

"The grand maxim of learning is to fix the mind on the right things. To put it in a paradoxical form, to know what to forget is the secret of learning well."—Rev E Thring.

"It needed the authority of the Postmaster-General to start the experiment which is being made of the use of postage stamps as an incentive to thrift; but, for some time back, postage stamps have been largely used without official sanction at all—none, indeed, being needed —for, in a sense, as practical and in all respects as useful an end. They have been the passport of a system of education which, although conducted in writing, has yet been attended with the results that follow oral teaching, for the persons who have taken advantage of the scheme have found themselves qualified to go successfully through the ordeal of examination.

"There is not a district within the limits of the United Kingdom where the letter-carrier cannot be met on his daily round He, then, is the janitor of this singular Educational Institution. Wherever he is to be found the work can be carried on, and is actually being carried on. There are men and women in large centres of population who desire to continue their studies, but whose spare time does not correspond with the hours at which class-teaching is usually given; and to their case, as well as to that of the inmates of distant and lonely houses, the plan of education by post addresses itself. Moreover, there is a class of persons who, having left school, are willing enough, and possibly eager, to continue their studies and keep abreast of the progress of thought, but who shrink from encountering the attrition of the class-room. To them also this system is a ready and open door leading to honest and carefully directed private study.

"The solitary student is the individual to whom education by post chiefly commends itself, and it will be understood that the instructive value of the process becomes very apparent to the pupil on the return of the written exercise, with the notes and explanatory remarks of the teacher."—*Leeds Mercury.*

ORAL CLASSES AND PRIVATE TUITION.

LAST MONTH CLASSES AT CAMBRIDGE.

Private Tuition may be obtained in London and Cambridge at any time of the year. Oral Classes are formed at Burlington House, Cambridge, for Recapitulation prior to all Matriculation, Inter. Arts, and B A. Examinations.

The charge for private tuition is 4s to 5s. per hour, according to the subject and examination Two in a class at three-fourths this rate; three at two-thirds; four at one-half. Where possible and advantageous, students are worked together if they so desire.

During school vacations and the last month before B.A., students may reside at Cambridge and take lessons in each subject daily for two guineas a week. Private rooms and board can be provided for a limited number of pupils at one guinea a week, preference being given to Correspondents, who will also be allowed some reduction in fees if they enter for a complete course of oral revision.

Oral tuition is given by the following graduates —

J. LOCKEY, Esq , M.A. London.

(*Had 27 Successful Private Pupils at the B.A. Exams.* 1886 *and* 1887.)

Author of Glossaries to *Alfred's Orosius*, Translations of *Battle of Maldon*, *Alfred's Orosius*, *King Edmund*, *Pro Cluentio*, &c.

G. W HILL, Esq., B Sc. (Hons), M B. (Hons), First-Class Honours at Inter. B.Sc., Sub-Examiner of Lond Univ.

Miss BRAND, B.A. (for Ladies); First-Class Degree, 1884, Matriculation Honours, 1883, Author of *Intermediate Latin*, *Vocabularies and Exam. Papers to Cicero pro Cluentio*.

V. BRANFORD, Esq., M.A., University Prizeman, First-Class Honours, Author of *A Zoological Classification*, &c.

B. J. HAYES, Esq , B.A. Lond , First in First-Class Honours in Classics both at Inter. and Final; Editor of *Homer's Iliad VI.*; Author of *Matric Latin*; *Vocabularies to Sallust's Catiline*, Translation of *Xenophon's Oeconomicus*, Jointly of *Inter. Greek*.

W. F MASOM, Esq., B.A., Lond , First-Class Honours (Classics) at B A., Double Honours (French and English) at Inter. Arts, Second in Honours at Matric , University Exhibitioner; Editor of *Homer's Odyssey, XVII.*; Author of *Vocabularies to Aeneid I.*; A Translation of *The Epistles of Horace*; *A Synopsis of Roman and Grecian History*.

F. RYLAND, Esq., M.A., Second in First-Class Honours (Mental and Moral Science, &c.), Author of a *Manual of Psychology and Ethics for Lond. B.A. and B.Sc.*, &c.,

Assisted, for Matriculation, by W. LIGHTFOOT, Esq., B.A., and J. DUNCAN, Esq., B A.

The above, with the exception of one or two giving private tuition in special subjects, are among the regular corresponding College Tutors.

University Correspondence College.

TUTORS.

M.A. Camb. and Lond Univs., Wrangler, Exhibitioner, Scholar, and Goldsmith Prizeman.

M.A. London (Classics and Anglo-Saxon).
Had 27 Successful Private Pupils at the B A Exams. 1886 *and* 1887)

B.A. London, Double Honours in French and German (1st Class)

M.A. Double 1st Class Hons , late Examiner.

B.Sc. (Hons.), M B. (Hons.), First-Class Honours at Inter. B.Sc. and Prelim. Sci., Sub-Examiner of Lond Univ.

M.A. London, Gold Medallist in Classics.

B.A. Lond., Hons in English, French, German, and Classics (First Class); Div. I, Class II, Classical Tripos, Cambridge

B.Sc., F.C.S., F.I.C., Honours Graduate of London

M A. Lond. (Mathematics), and Cambridge Wrangler.

B.A., First-Class Degree, 1884, Matriculation Honours, 1883.

M.A. University Prizeman, First-Class Honours.

B.A. Lond., First-Class Honours (Classics) at B A., Double Honours (French and English) at Inter. Arts; Second in Honours at Matric.; University Exhibitioner.

B.Sc. Lond, First in First-Class Honours both at Inter. and Final.

B.A. Lond., First in First-Class Honours in Classics both at Inter. and Final.

M.A., First-Class Honours (Mental and Moral Science, etc.), Author of a Manual of Psychology and Ethics for Lond. B.A. and B.Sc.

LL.B., First in First-Class Honours, Jurisprudence and Roman Law, and Honoursman in Common Law and Equity.

And other Honours Graduates of London in special subjects

The Tutorial Series.

XENOPHON'S OECONOMICUS.

A TRANSLATION.

BY

B. J. HAYES, B.A. (LOND.),

FIRST IN FIRST CLASS CLASSICAL HONOURS BOTH AT INTERMEDIATE AND FINAL B.A.

TUTOR OF

PUBLISHED AT THE
UNIVERSITY CORRESPONDENCE COLLEGE OFFICE,
CAMBRIDGE.

University Correspondence Students, use for Text and Notes, Holden's edition of *Xenophon's Oeconomicus.* (6s. Macmillan.)

Test Papers have been prepared suitable for B.A , and can be had post free. 2s., from W. B. Clive, Cambridge.

Full list of works prepared for London University Examinations post free on application.

XENOPHON'S OECONOMICUS.

I.

I ONCE heard him discoursing also on household management as follows:—

Tell me, Critobulus, he said, is not household management the name of a craft, such as medicine, metallurgy, and carpentry?

Yes, I think so, said Critobulus.

Then, just as we could say what the function of each of these arts is, can we in the same way in the case of household management also say what its function is?

At any rate, said Critobulus, it seems that it is the business of a good manager of a household to govern his own house well.

And another's house too, I suppose, said Socrates, if a man were to entrust it to him? Would he not be able, if he were willing, to govern it well, in the same way as his own? For he who is skilled in carpentry would likewise be able to do also for another whatever he could do for himself, and the manager of a household too in like manner.

I think so, Socrates.

Is it possible, said Socrates, for one skilled in this art, even if he himself should not possess property, to earn wages for managing another's house, just as for building it?

Yes, assuredly, said Critobulus, and he would earn higher wages too, if on taking over an estate he could both do all that is needful and by securing a surplus increase the estate.

In what then do we consider a household to consist?

Is it identical with the dwelling-house, or do all those things which a man possesses outside the house form part of the household?

It seems to me, said Critobulus, that even if they should not be in the same city as the possessor, all things which a man possesses belong to the household.

So then some even possess enemies?

Yes, assuredly; and some possess many.

Then shall we say that the enemies too are their property?

Yet it would be ridiculous, said Critobulus, if he who increases a man's enemies should moreover earn wages for this too.

This follows, you know, from our decision that a man's household was identical with his possessions.

It is assuredly so, said Critobulus, with regard to whatever good thing one possesses. As to any evil thing, I most certainly do not call that a possession.

But you seem to call those things possessions which profit the individual.

Just so, he said; while those things that are injurious I look upon as a nuisance rather than as property.

Well, and suppose a man after buying a horse does not know how to use it, but falls down from it and receives an injury, is not the horse property to him?

No, not at least on the supposition that property is a good thing

Neither is his land then property to any man who so cultivates it as to lose by doing so.

Assuredly his land is not property, if instead of supporting him it brings him starvation.

Therefore in the same way in the case of sheep also, if any one through not understanding the treatment of sheep should suffer loss, the sheep would not be property to this man?

No, I do not think they would.

So you, as it seems, look upon those things that profit a man as property, but those which injure him as no property.

[illegible]

Then although they are the same, they are property to him who knows how to use each of them, but to him who does not know, they are no property; as, for instance, flutes are property to one who knows how to play tolerably well, but to one who does not know are nothing more than useless pebbles, unless indeed he should sell them. This then is clear to us, that if they sell them the flutes are property, and if they do not sell them, but possess them, they are no property to those who do not themselves know how to use them.

Well, Socrates, our argument at any rate is progressing consistently, since it has been decided that those things which profit are property. For the flutes, if they be not sold, are no property, for they are of no service; but if they are sold, they are property.

In answer to this Socrates said: Yes, if he knows how to sell them. But if he should sell them again for that which he did not know how to use, even if sold they are no property, at least according to your argument.

You seem to say, Socrates, that not even money is property, unless a man know how to use it.

And you too appear to me to acknowledge this, that those things by which a man can be profited are property. So if a man should make such use of his money as to purchase a woman, for instance, and because of her should fare worse as regards his body, worse as regards his soul, and worse as regards his household, how could his money yet be of service to him?

In no way; unless indeed we shall say that even the so-called henbane is property, though under its influence they who eat it become mad.

So then, unless a man know how to use it, let him put money so far out of consideration, Critobulus, that it count not as property. But as to friends, if a man knows how to use them so as to derive profit from them, what shall we say that they are?

Property, assuredly, said Critobulus; and much more so than cattle, if only they are more serviceable than cattle.

Then enemies too are property, at least according to

your argument, to him who can derive profit from his enemies

Yes, I think so.

Then it is the part of a good manager to know how to use even his enemies, so as to derive profit from his enemies.

Most decidedly.

For as a matter of fact you see, Critobulus, he said, how many estates both of private persons and of despots have been increased by means of war.

Now another point, Socrates; for these things seem to me to be well argued, said Critobulus What conclusion do we draw as to this, when we see that some men have skill and opportunity to enable them by exerting themselves to increase their estates, but perceive that they will not do this, and therefore see that their skill is unprofitable to them? What conclusion but this: that their skill is not property to these men any more than their possessions?

Are you, Critobulus, trying to argue with me about slaves? said Socrates.

Assuredly I am not, he said, but of those, some at least of whom are held to be of quite the highest rank, whom I see to possess skill, some in warlike, others in peaceful arts, but to be unwilling to employ this skill for this very reason (as I think) that they have no masters.

And how, said Socrates, can it be that they have no masters, if, though desirous to be happy and anxious to do that from which they will get good, they are after all prevented from doing this by their rulers?

And pray who are these, said Critobulus, who, though invisible, rule them?

Nay, assuredly, said Socrates, they are not invisible, but very visible indeed. Nor can you fail to see that they are certainly the worst of rulers if you consider idleness to be a vice, and effeminacy of soul, and negligence. And there are other guileful mistresses pretending to be pleasures, that is to say, dice-playing and bad company; and as time goes on it becomes clear to those very men who were deceived that these, which when they get the upper hand hinder them from lucrative occupations, were really pains covered with a crust of pleasure.

Yet others too, Socrates, he said, are not by these hindered from working, but are wholly bent on working and on procuring an income, but they nevertheless waste their estates, and are hampered for want of means.

For these also are slaves, said Socrates, and of very hard masters too; some of gluttony, others of lust, others of drunkenness, others of foolish and expensive ambitions, which exercise so cruel a sway over the men on whom they gain a hold that, so long as they see them in their prime and able to work, they compel them to bring whatever they earn and spend it on their own lusts, but when they perceive that they are on account of their advanced age unable to work, they leave them to grow old in wretchedness, and attempt to treat others as slaves in turn. But it is no less necessary, Critobulus, to carry on the fight for freedom against these enemies than against those who attempt to enslave us by force of arms Now, ere this, enemies noble and upright in disposition have, after reducing men to slavery, brought very many to their senses, and compelled them to improve and have made them live at greater ease for the future; but tyrants of the former kind never cease harassing the bodies of men, and their souls and their households, as long as they have dominion over them.

II.

Critobulus. therefore, hereupon spoke to this effect. Now on this subject I am well assured that I have heard your opinion at sufficient length, and on examining myself I think I find that I am fairly well able to control such passions, so that if you should advise me what to do to increase my estate, I do not think that it is by these passions which you call masters, that I should be hindered. So without hesitation give me what good advice you can; or have you concluded with regard to us, Socrates, that we are rich enough, and do we seem to you to stand in no need of additional property?

Well, I for my part, said Socrates, if you include me, think I stand in no need at all of additional property, but that I am rich enough; you, however, Critobulus, seem to me to be utterly poor, and most assuredly at times I absolutely pity you.

And Critobulus laughed and said: Why, by the gods above us, Socrates, how much do you think your possessions would fetch if offered for sale, and how much would mine?

I think, said Socrates, that if I found a good purchaser, my house and all my belongings would, without any difficulty, fetch twenty pounds; while I know for a certainty that yours would fetch more than a hundred times as much as that.

And yet, though you know this, you consider that you have no need of additional property, but pity me for my poverty?

Yes, he said, for my possessions are great enough to provide me with those things which suffice for me; but as for your style of living which you have adopted, and your position, even if thrice as much as you now possess should accrue to you, I think that not even so would you possess sufficient.

How now can that be? said Critobulus.

[Socrates expressed his opinion:] In the first place I see that you are under the necessity of offering many large sacrifices, or else I expect that neither gods nor men would tolerate you; next you have to receive many guests, and them too with magnificence; and again you must entertain and benefit your fellow citizens, or else lack supporters. And I moreover perceive that, under present circumstances, the city too orders you to pay heavy contributions, such as the keeping of horses, the payment of choruses, and trainers, and presidencies, and in the event of war breaking out, I know that they will impose on you the equipment of a ship and the payment of property tax to an extent that will prove no light burden to you. And on whatever occasion you may appear to perform any of these offices inefficiently, I know that the Athenians will punish you no less severely than if they detected you stealing their own property. And in addition to this I see that you think yourself rich, and are indifferent about making money but give your mind to childish pursuits as if you were free to do so. For which reasons I pity you, for fear you should suffer some irreparable evil, and be reduced to great want. And I know, as also do you, that if I too should need anything further, there are those who would assist me, so that by providing very little they would make my life overflow with plenty, while your friends, having means far more adequate than you to their own style of living, than you (I mean) have to yours, yet look to you to receive benefits at your hands.

And Critobulus said: I cannot gainsay this, Socrates; but it is time for you to make provision on my behalf that I become not pitiable in reality.

On hearing this, Socrates said: And do you not think, Critobulus, that you are acting in a strange manner with regard to yourself, in that a little while ago, when I said that I was rich, you laughed at me as though I did not even know what wealth was, and did not rest until you proved me wrong, and had made me confess that I did not possess even a hundredth part of your property; whereas now you bid me make provision on your behalf, and take care that you become not altogether poor in fact?

The reason is, Socrates, that I see that you know one particular method of enrichment, namely, how to produce a surplus. Thus I expect that he who makes a surplus from a small income, would from a large income very easily produce a large surplus.

Do you then not remember that recent incident in our talk, when you did not give me leave even to breathe a word against your statement that to him who does not know how to use horses, the horses would be no property, and so with land, or sheep, or money, or anything else which a man did not know how to use? Incomes, then, arise from such things as these; but how do you suppose that I should know how to use any of them, when I never possessed any one of them at all?

But we agreed that, even if a man should happen to have no property, nevertheless some skill in household management was possible. What then prevents you too from having this skill?

The same cause, assuredly, which would prevent a man

from being skilled in playing, if he himself were not possessed of flutes, and no other man allowed him to learn on his; so the case stands with me too with regard to household management. For neither did I myself possess property as an instrument to learn from, nor did another ever provide me with his property to administer, except that just now you wanted to do so. But, of course, those who begin learning to play spoil the lyres at the same time: and I, if I were to undertake to learn from your estate to manage a household, should perhaps utterly ruin your estate

In answer to this, Critobulus said · You are trying very hard in my case, Socrates, to avoid giving me any help towards carrying on my every-day affairs with greater ease.

Oh no, said Socrates, I assuredly am not; and as far as I can I will expound the matter to you, and very readily too. Now, supposing you had come to fetch fire and I had none by me, you would not, I think, have blamed me if I had directed you to another place whence it would be possible for you to obtain it; and supposing that I had no water for you on your requesting me for it, if I had led you for it too to some other place, I know that you would not have found fault with me for this either; and supposing you wish to learn accomplishments from me, if I should point out to you some much more skilful in accomplishments than I, and such as would feel under an obligation to you if you would take lessons from them, for what would you still blame me if I so acted?

For nothing, Socrates, at least not with justice.

I therefore, Critobulus, point out to you others much more skilful than myself in these subjects in which you are now eager to take lessons from me And I confess that I have felt an interest in the question as to who in the city are best versed in each subject. For having formerly observed that by means of the same occupations some were in absolute need and others thoroughly well off, I was struck with astonishment, and the reason for this seemed to me to be worthy of investigation. And I found on consideration that this came to pass quite naturally. For I began to see that those who carried on these pursuits at random were losers, but I noticed that those who gave heed to them with earnest purpose accomplished them more quickly and easily and to greater profit. From which facts I think that you too, if you wished, might take a lesson, and, if Heaven did not oppose, become quite a shrewd man of business.

III.

On hearing this, Critobulus said: Now in truth I will never let you go, Socrates, before you demonstrate to me what you promised in the presence of these friends here.

What then, Critobulus, said Socrates, if I demonstrate to you first that some at a great expense build unserviceable houses, and others for much less build such as contain all that is wanted? Shall I seem in this to be giving you one particular specimen of household matters?

Yes, most certainly, said Critobulus.

And what if I, after this, exhibit that which follows on this, that some who possess goods and chattels in very large quantities and of various kinds, and are unable to use them when they require, and do not know if they have them safe, are even on account of these very things themselves much annoyed, and annoy their household much; while others, though they possess no more but rather less than the former, have at once ready for use whatever they require.

But what now is the reason of this, Socrates, save that by the former everything has been cast down at random, but by the latter each article has been arranged in its place?

Yes, assuredly, said Socrates, and each article has been well arranged, not just in a place at random, but where it is convenient.

In this too, said Critobulus, you seem to me to be stating one point in household management.

What then, he said, if again I exhibit to you servants at one place almost all bound and often trying to run off, and at another place free and willing both to work and to stay? Shall I not seem to exhibit to you in this also a feat of household management well worth seeing?

Yes, assuredly, said Critobulus, and exceedingly so.

And if I show you men cultivating similar farms, some saying that they have been ruined by farming and are in need, and others that in plenty and prosperity they have everything they require from their husbandry?

Yes, assuredly, said Critobulus. For perhaps the latter are spending money not only on what they ought, but also on things which injure the master and the household.

There are perhaps some, said Socrates, of this description too. But I am not speaking of these, but of those who have not anything to spend even on necessaries, though they profess to be farming.

And what can be the cause of this, Socrates?

I will take you, said Socrates, to see these men too; and when you see them you will, I expect, learn the whole matter.

Most assuredly, he said, so far as I can.

Then you must make trial of yourself, as to whether you will gain knowledge by seeing them. But at present I know that to view tragedies and comedies you both rise very early and go a very long distance, and earnestly urge me to go with you to the sight; but you never invited me to anything like that I mentioned.

I therefore appear ridiculous in your eyes, Socrates.

And assuredly, he said, much more ridiculous in your own. And if I show you that from horsemanship too some have come to want necessaries, and others through horsemanship are even very well off and at the same time glory in their profit?

Why yes, I too see and know these men of either sort, and not one bit the more do I become one of the gainers.

No, for you look at them as you do tragic and comic actors, not I suppose that you may become a poet, but that you may receive pleasure from what you see and hear. And this perhaps is rightly so, for you do not want to become a poet; but as you are compelled to employ horsemanship, do you not think that you are foolish if you do not consider how you may be practised in this work, especially as the same objects are both good for use and profitable for sale?

Do you bid me be a horse-breaker, Socrates?

No, assuredly; no more than to buy and train husbandmen from boyhood. But there seems to me to be some periods in the life both of horses and of men, which are not only of present service, but continue to improve. And I can show that some so treat their wedded wives also as to have them as fellow workers in helping to increase their estates, and that others treat them in a way in which most of those who do so bring themselves to ruin.

And for this, Socrates, are we to blame the man or the woman?

If a sheep is ill-conditioned, said Socrates, we generally blame the shepherd, and generally if a horse is vicious we accuse the rider; but in the case of a wife, if though instructed in good conduct by her husband, she manages badly, perhaps the wife would deservedly bear the blame. But if he does not teach her what is right and good, then would not the husband deservedly bear the blame, if he should find her ignorant of such things? But, Critobulus, he continued, at all events tell us the whole truth, for we are all friends here. Is there any one else to whom you entrust more of your important affairs than you do to your wife?

No one, he said.

But is there anyone with whom you have fewer discussions than you do with your wife?

If not so, certainly there are not many, he said.

But you married her when she was quite a young girl, and when she had seen and heard as little of things as possible.

Certainly.

Therefore it is much more remarkable if she should understand any of the things which she ought to say or do, than if she should make a mistake

But did those, Socrates, whom you declare to possess good wives, themselves train them?

There is nothing like looking into it. And I will introduce Aspasia also to you, who will show you all these things more skilfully than I. And I think that a wife, if she is a good partner in the household, is quite equivalent to the husband in utility. For it is through the husband's exertions for the most part that possessions come to the house, but they are most of them spent by the wife's dispensation; and when this is well performed the estates increase, but when ill performed the estates diminish. And I think that I could show you those who ply each of the other trades too in a manner worthy of note, if you consider that you need any further argument.

IV.

But why need you show them all, Socrates? said Critobulus. For neither is it easy to procure workmen of the proper sort in all the trades, nor is it possible to become skilled in them; but whichever of the sciences seem noblest, and such as it would be most suitable for me to engage in, show me these; and not only them, but those who pursue them; and do you too, as far as you can, help me in this by your instructions.

Now you say well, Critobulus, said he. For, moreover, the so-called mechanical arts are exclaimed against, and are besides altogether held in disrepute by the states, and deservedly so. For they utterly ruin the constitutions of the workmen and the overseers, by obliging them to be seated and to keep indoors, and in the case of some to spend the day by the fire. And while their bodies are enervated, their souls too become much less strong. And the so-called mechanical arts, moreover, involve to a great degree lack of leisure to attend also to friends and to politics. So that such men seem bad too for their friends to deal with, and to be bad defenders of their country. And in some of the states, and especially in those which seem to be successful in war, it is not even lawful for any of the citizens to ply mechanical arts.

But now what sort of art do you counsel us to practise, Socrates?

Can we, said Socrates, possibly be ashamed of imitating the king of the Persians? For they say that he considers agriculture and the art of war to rank among the most honourable and most necessary occupations, and that he gives strict attention to both these.

And when Critobulus heard this, he said: Do you believe even this, Socrates, that the king of the Persians gives any share of his attention to agriculture?

Looking at the matter in this way, Critobulus, said Socrates, we shall perhaps learn if he gives it a share of his attention. For we are agreed that he gives strict attention to matters of war, because he has given orders to the governors of the several nations from whom he receives tribute as to the number of horse soldiers, archers, slingers, and targeteers to which he must assign rations. This number must be sufficient both to keep in subjection the tribes ruled by him, and in the case of an invasion by enemies to defend the country. And in addition to these he keeps garrisons in the citadels, and the officer to whom this duty has been assigned gives the guards their rations. And the king, year by year, holds a review of the mercenaries, and of the others to whom orders have been given to be under arms, at the same time also massing where the so-called muster of forces is all his men except those in the citadels. And he himself reviews the troops that are about his own household, but sends trusty men to inspect those stationed at a distance And as many of the commanders of garrisons and field officers and satraps as are found to have the appointed number complete, and who produce the men provided with proper horses and armour, these officers he both raises to the ranks of honour and enriches with handsome presents. But whatever officers he finds either careless of the garrisons or making unjust gains, these he punishes severely, and deposing them from their office, he put others in charge. So as he does this with regard to the matters of war, he seems to us unquestionably to give them his attention. And, moreover, he himself also investigates as much of the country as he surveys on riding through, and he sends trustworthy men, and inspects as much as he does not himself survey. And as many of the governors as he perceives able to show their land thickly inhabited, and the ground well tilled and stocked with the trees which the several countries produce and with crops, to these he gives other land in addition, and honours them with presents and rewards them with places of honour. But all those whose land he sees untilled and thinly inhabitated, either through cruelty or violence or carelessness, them he punishes and deposes from their office, and appoints other governors In so doing does he seem to take less care that the land shall be well tilled by the inhabitants than that it shall be well guarded by the garrisons? And, moreover, those put in charge by him for either purpose are not the same, but some govern the inhabitants and labourers, and collect tribute from them, while others are in command of the armed garrisons. And if the commander of the garrison does not afford sufficient protection to the country, he who governs the populace and has charge of the industries brings an accusation against the commander of the garrison because they cannot work for the want of protection. And if, when the commander of the garrison secures peace for the industries, the governor can only show a land thinly inhabited and untilled, the commander of the garrison in turn brings a charge against him. For, moreover, those who till the land badly generally neither support the garrison, nor are able to pay the tribute. But wherever a satrap is appointed, he pays attention to both these matters.

Hereupon Critobulus said: Well then, Socrates, if the king does this, he seems to me to give no less attention to the affairs of agriculture than to those of war.

And moreover, in addition to this, said Socrates, in whatever places he dwells, and to whatever places he pays visits, he attends to these matters, that the gardens which are called *paradisi* may be full of all such goodly and serviceable plants as the land is wont to produce, and in these he himself passes most of his time, when the season of the year does not prevent.

Assuredly, Socrates, said Critobulus, it needs must be, therefore, that he at the same time takes care that there, where he himself passes his time, the parks shall be ornamented as beautifully as possible with trees and all the other beautiful things which the land produces.

And some declare, Critobulus, said Socrates, that also whenever the king gives presents he calls in first those who have proved brave in war, because it is of no avail to plough much land unless there be men to defend it; and next those who cultivate the lands best and make them productive, for he says that not even the valiant would be able to live unless there were tillers of the soil And Cyrus, who has proved a most glorious prince, is also said once to have told those summoned to receive their presents that he himself might fairly receive the gifts awarded to both; for he said that he excelled both in cultivating land and in defending that which was cultivated

Well then, Socrates, said Critobulus, Cyrus, if he said this, even prided himself upon making the lands productive and cultivating them no less than upon being a man of war

Yes, and it seems too, said Socrates, that Cyrus, if he had lived, would have proved a very good ruler; and he has given many proofs of this, and especially by the fact that when he was marching to fight with his brother for the kingdom, it is said that no one deserted from Cyrus to the king, but many tens of thousands deserted from the king to Cyrus. And I think that this too is a great proof of a ruler's merit, if men willingly obey him, and are ready to remain by his side in difficulties. And with him his friends both fought while he was alive and died when he died, all except Ariaeus, fighting for his body. But Ariaeus happened to have been stationed on the left wing. Now this Cyrus is said to have shown favour to Lysander when he came bringing him the gifts from the allies, both in other ways (as Lysander himself declared in his narrative to a friend at Megara), and he said that he showed him the park at Sardis And as Lysander was admiring it for the grandeur of its trees, the uniform distances at which they were planted, the straightness of the rows of the trees, the beautiful regularity of all the angles, and the number and sweetness of the odours that accompanied them as they walked about, as (I say) he was admiring these things, he said, "Truly. Cyrus, though I admire all these things for their beauty, yet I marvel much more at the man who measured out and arranged each of them for you." And when Cyrus heard this he was pleased and said: "Well then, Lysander, I both measured out and arranged all of them; and there are some of them," he added, "which I also planted myself" And Lysander related how he looked at him and beheld both the beauty of the garments which he was wearing and perceived their scent, and the beauty of his chains and armlets and of the rest of the dress which he was wearing, and said: "What do you mean, Cyrus? For did you plant any of these with your own hands?" And Cyrus in reply said: "Are you astonished at this, Lysander? I swear to you by Mithras that whenever in good health I never dined before putting myself into a perspiration by attending either to military or to agricultural matters or by continually pursuing some one object of ambition" And Lysander said that when he heard this he in fact seized him by the hand and replied: "You seem to me, Cyrus, to be justly prosperous, for your prosperity is equalled by good qualities."

V.

And I narrate this, Critobulus, said Socrates, because not even those who are quite well-to-do can abstain from agriculture. For attention to it seems to be at the same time a luxury and a means of increasing their estate, and a training of their bodies so that they have strength to do whatever becomes a free man For, in the first place, the earth produces for those who till it those things on which men live, and in addition it produces those things on which they live luxuriously withal; and next, it furnishes too, together with most delightful scents and sights, all those materials with which they deck altars and images, and with which they adorn themselves; and thirdly, it bears or nourishes many articles of food, for the art of cattle-breeding too is closely associated with agriculture, so that men can both appease the gods by sacrificing and supply their own wants. But though the earth furnishes her good things most ungrudgingly, she does not suffer men to obtain them with remissness, but accustoms them to endure both the cold of winter and the heat of summer. And in exercising some workers by their manual labour she gives them more strength, and others she hardens by their supervision of the labourers, causing them to rise early and compelling them to busy themselves zealously. For both in the country and in the town the most important matters are always fixed to a time. Again, if a man desires to defend his country on horseback, a country life provides the best keep for his horse; and if on foot, it renders the body active. And the earth helps one to a certain extent to take an additional interest in hunting by furnishing an easy supply of food for dogs and by maintaining at the same time beasts of the chase And while both horses and dogs are benefited by agriculture, they benefit the country in return—the horse by taking his master to his work of supervision in the morning and giving him the opportunity of leaving it late, and the dogs by keeping the wild beasts from destroying the crops and flocks and by helping to provide the necessary safety for lonely parts. And the earth also in some degree stimulates the labourers to defend the land under arms, too, by producing the crops in the open country for the strongest to take. And what art produces men better able to run, shoot, and leap than agriculture does? And what art makes greater returns to those who ply it? And what art welcomes its devotee more gladly, holding forth to him who approaches it the attainment of whatever he requires? And what art receives strangers more ungrudgingly? And where is there greater facility for passing the winter with plenty of fire and with warm baths than in the country? And where is it more pleasant to pass the summer with streams and breezes and shade than a-field? And what other art provides fitter first-fruits for the gods or supplies more perfect festivals? And what art is more agreeable to servants and more pleasant for a wife, or more longed for by children, or more delightful to friends? To me it seems to be astonishing if any free man possesses either any object more pleasing than this or has found any occupation more pleasing than this, or more conducive to the means of life. And, moreover, the earth kindly teaches justice also to those who can learn, in that to those that treat her best she does most good in return. And if also it ever so happens that those who are employed in agriculture and are trained to vigorous and manly habits are kept from their occupations by a massing of armies, they can go to the lands of those who are hindering them and seize booty on which they will subsist. And often it is even safer in war to seek one's food with arms than with the implements of husbandry. And agriculture also helps in training men to render mutual assistance. For it is necessary both to march against the enemy with the help of men, and it is with men's help that the cultivation of the land is carried on. He, therefore, who will be a good farmer must make his labourers both zealous and ready to obey, and he who leads men against the enemy must accomplish the same thing both by rewarding those who do what brave men ought to do and by punishing the undisciplined. And also it is frequently no less necessary for the farmer to encourge his labourers than the general his soldiers; and slaves also need good prospects no less than free men, but even more, in order that they may be willing to stay And he, too, said well who declared that agriculture was the mother and nurse of the other arts For so long as agriculture succeeds, the other arts also flourish; but whenever the earth is compelled to lie waste, the other arts, too, are almost extinguished both by land and by sea.

And Critobulus on hearing this, said: I think indeed, Socrates, that in this you say well; but inasmuch as most matters of agriculture are such as cannot be foreseen by man, for hail and sometimes frost and drought and excessive rains and mildew and other things often destroy what has been excellently devised and wrought, and sometimes a plague comes and carries off sheep, too, that have been most carefully reared.

And when Socrates heard this he said: But I thought, Critobulus, that you were aware that the gods are no less supreme over the operations of husbandry than over those of war? And I think you see those engaged in war before they commence hostilities appeasing the gods and consulting them by means of sacrifices and omens both as to what they should do and as to what they should not do. And do you think it less necessary to propitiate the gods with regard to the operations of husbandry? For you may rest assured, said he, that the wise do service to the gods on behalf both of succulent and dry fruits, and of cattle, and horses, and sheep, and, in fact, on behalf of all their possessions.

VI.

Now in this, Socrates, you seem to me, he said, to speak well, bidding us to try to begin every work with the gods' assistance, on the ground that the gods are supreme no less over works of peace than over those of war. We will endeavour, then, to carry this out in practice. But do you, beginning from the point at which you left off speaking to us about agriculture, endeavour to discuss thoroughly those matters which appertain to this subject; for even now I think that after hearing all you said I already see somewhat more clearly than before what I must do to get my living.

Well, said Socrates, suppose now that we first recapitulate all we have gone over and agreed on, in order that, if we by any means can, we may endeavour to discuss the rest too thus in agreement.

It is certainly pleasant, said Critobulus, when partners in business go through their accounts without disagreement, and it is equally so when those who are partners in arguments discuss harmoniously all the subjects of their discourse.

Household management, then, said Socrates, seemed to us to be the name of a certain science, and this science was seen to be that by which men can increase their households; and we saw that a household was identical with the whole of a man's property, and we said that property included all that was profitable for his livelihood; and all such things as a man knew how to use were found to be profitable. Now it seemed to us impossible that a man should learn all the sciences, but that we should join with the states in condemning the so-called mechanical arts, both because they seem to be injurious to the body and because they enervate the soul. And we said that it would be the clearest proof of this, if, on the invasion of the country by an enemy, a man were to make the agricultural labourers and the artisans sit apart, and were to ask each class separately whether they approved of defending the land or of surrendering the open country and guarding the walls. For in that case we thought that those engaged in the country would vote for defending it, but the artisans for not fighting but for sitting still without incurring toil or dangers, just as they have been brought up to do. And we came to the conclusion that for a man of good breeding and character the best employment and science was agriculture, by means of which men provide themselves with necessaries. For this employment seemed both easiest to learn and most pleasant to practise, and to make their bodies most comely and strong, and to be farthest from leaving their thoughts no leisure for giving a share of their attention to friends and country. And agriculture seemed to us to help somewhat towards provoking men to bravery by producing and feeding outside the fortified places the necessaries of life for the labourers. And on this account this mode of life was seen to be most honoured by the states because it seems to furnish citizens endowed with the greatest bravery and best affected towards the commonwealth.

And Critobulus replied. I think I am quite sufficiently convinced, Socrates, that our life derives culture, bravery, and pleasure to the highest degree from agriculture; but with regard to what you said about examining the causes why some so farm as to obtain from their farming abundantly what they require, while others so labour that their farming does not profit them, I think I should also be glad to hear from you an account of each of these cases, in order that we may pursue that course which is advantageous and avoid that which is harmful.

Suppose then, Critobulus, said Socrates, that I narrate to you from the beginning how I once met a man who seemed to me to be one of those men in whose case this name of man of good breeding and character is justly applied.

I should be very glad, said Critobulus, to hear this, as I am even myself desirous of becoming worthy of this name.

Then I will also tell you, said Socrates, how I came to

the consideration of it. Now as regards good carpenters, good smiths, good painters, good sculptors, and everything else of the kind, a very short time sufficed me to go round and see those works of theirs which have been commonly considered excellent. But in order that I might observe those also who had this revered name of man of good breeding and character as to what they did to have a claim to be so called, my soul greatly desired to meet one of them. And, in the first place, because good breeding was attached to good character, I used to accost everyone of good breeding whom I saw, and endeavoured to gain information, to try if haply I might see good character united with good breeding. But it was not so after all, but I thought I discovered that some men goodly in outward appearance were altogether depraved in mind. So I resolved to leave the goodliness of outward appearance, and go in quest of one of those who are called men of good breeding and character. So when I was constantly told that Ischomachus was styled a man of good breeding and character by all, both men and women, strangers and citizens, I resolved to endeavour to meet this man.

VII.

So seeing him on one occasion sitting in the cloister of Zeus the Releaser, as he seemed to me to be at leisure, I went up to him and, sitting by his side, said: Why, Ischomachus, is it not your general custom to sit at leisure? For I see you, in general at least, either engaged in something, or not sitting quite idle in the market place.

No, nor would you have seen me so now, Socrates, said Ischomachus, had I not agreed to wait some strangers here.

But when you are not engaged in some such thing, I said, in Heaven's name where do you pass your time, and what do you do? For I am really very anxious to learn from you what it is you do that you are called a man of good breeding and character; for you certainly do not pass your time indoors, nor does the condition of your body present that appearance.

And Ischomachus laughed at the question, "What is it

you do that you are called a man of good breeding and character?" and (as far as I could tell) was pleased, and said: Well, I do not know if when people talk to you about me they call me by this name, for certainly when they challenge me for an exchange of the duty of fitting out a trireme or providing a chorus, he continued, no one seeks the man of good breeding and character; but, said he, they undoubtedly summon me into court by calling me Ischomachus, adding my father's name. Now as to the question you were asking me, Socrates, he added: I am by no means wont to stay indoors. For, in fact, my wife even alone is quite competent to manage matters at home.

But I should be very glad, Ischomachus, I said, to learn this too from you, whether you yourself trained your wife to be what she should be, or received her when she had learnt from her father and mother to manage those matters which concern her.

And what could she have learnt, Socrates, he said, when I received her? for she came to me when not yet fifteen years old, and during the time preceding that had lived under strict surveillance, in order that she might see as little as possible, hear as little as possible, and speak as little as possible For do you not think that one must be content if she came merely knowing how to make a garment if she had wool given her, and having observed how the spinning tasks are apportioned to handmaids? For certainly, he added, as to what concerns the appetite, Socrates, she had been thoroughly well brought up, and that seems to me to be the chief point of instruction both for a man and for a woman.

But in other matters, I said, did you yourself, Ischomachus, train your wife to be competent to attend to those matters which concern her?

Yes, said Ischomachus, but in good truth not before I both offered sacrifice and prayed that the result might be that I should teach and she should learn those things which were of the greatest advantage to us both.

Then your wife too, I said, joined with you in sacrificing and in praying for these same blessings?

That she certainly did, said Ischomachus, with many promises to the gods to become what she ought to be, and she gave sure signs that she would not disregard her instructions.

In Heaven's name, Ischomachus, I said, tell me what you first began to teach her, as I would more gladly hear you narrating this than if you should tell me of the most glorious contest in athletics or horse-racing.

And Ischomachus answered: Well, Socrates, as soon as she had become submissive to me, and felt sufficiently at home to carry on a conversation, I began to question her somewhat in this fashion: "Tell me, wife, if you have already perceived for what purpose I took you and your parents gave you to me? For I know that there was no necessity, but each of us might have lived in wedlock with someone else, and this is evident to you. But when I considered on my own account, and your parents on yours, whom each of us might take as the best partner of board and bed, I chose you, and also your parents, according as they could, apparently chose me. So if Heaven shall ever grant that children be born to us, we will then take into consideration with regard to them how we shall educate them as well as possible; for this advantage, too, is ours in common, to obtain helpmates and sustainers of our old age of the best kind possible; but now, you see, this house is ours in common For, whereas I from time to time pay into the common fund all that I have, you once for all invested in the common fund all that you brought And we have not this to calculate, namely, which of us has contributed the larger sum; but we must rest assured of this, that whichever of us is the better partner the same contributes that which is the more valuable." And my wife, Socrates, replied to me in answer to this: "And in what respect can I possibly help you? And what power have I? Nay, everything depends on you; and my mother said that my business was to be discreet" "Yes, most assuredly, my wife," I said, "for my father told me so, too. But it is in truth the part of discreet people, husband as well as wife, so to act that their possessions shall be in the best possible state and that as much else as possible shall accrue by fair and just means." "And what then," said my wife, "do you consider I could do to help in increasing our estate?" "Verily," I said, "in good truth try to do as well as possible those things of which the gods made you capable, and of which the law too approves." "And what then are these?" she said. "For my part," I said, "I think that they are not things of very small importance, unless indeed the queen-bee of the hive likewise presides over things of very small importance. For the gods, too, you know (so Ischomachus said he continued), seem to me, my wife, to have united this couple, which is called female and male, with much judgment, principally in order that it may be as beneficial as possible to itself in the matter of partnership. For, in the first place, this couple has been brought together with the intent that the species of living creatures may not die out; next, to the human race at least by means of this bond it becomes possible to obtain sustainers of their old age; and thirdly, too, the life of men is not like that of beasts passed in the open air, but clearly requires shelter. Those persons, however, who intend to have that which they may carry under shelter stand in need of one to carry on out-of-door occupations. For all these—ploughing and sowing and planting and grazing—are employments for the open air, and from these the necessaries of life are derived. And again, when these are brought under shelter, there is need of one to preserve them and to perform too those offices which indoor occupations require. And the nursing of new-born children requires indoor work, as also does the making of bread from corn; and so, too, does the production of clothing from wool. And since both kinds, indoor and outdoor occupations alike, require industry and attention (I continued), the God fitted their nature from birth, as it seems to me, that of the woman for the indoor occupations and cares, and that of the man for those out of doors For while He fitted the man's body and mind to be better able to endure cold and heat and travelling and warfare, thus allotting to him the outdoor occupations, the God seems to me, by making the woman's body naturally less capable of these things, to assign to her (so Ischomachus said he continued) the indoor occupations. And knowing that He implanted in and allotted to the woman the nurture of her new-born children, he gave to her also a larger share of love for her new-born babes than to the man. And as He also allotted to the woman the charge of what is brought into the house, the God, knowing that it is no bad thing for taking charge that the mind should be timid, gave to the woman also a larger share of fear than to the man. And knowing that he who has the outdoor employments will be obliged to provide protection also if anyone inflict an injustice, to him again He gave a larger share of courage. But because both alike ought to give and receive, He granted the faculties of memory and attention to both impartially. So that you can hardly determine whether the female or the male sex possesses them in a greater degree. And the God granted impartially to both to be self-restrained in matters in which they should be so, and made it possible that, whichever excelled, either the man or the woman, the same should receive also more of this good quality. And on account of the nature of both not being well adapted to all the same functions, they for this reason have greater need of each other, and the pair become more serviceable one to the other, one being competent wherein the other is deficient And we, my wife," I said, "knowing these functions which have been assigned to each of us by the God, must endeavour to accomplish as well as possible those duties which appertain to each of us. And the law too (so Ischomachus said he continued) gives its approval of this, in that it joins man and wife together. And just as the God made them partners in their children, so the law also appoints them partners of their household. And the law shows that those employments for which the God made each naturally more competent are praiseworthy. For it is more praiseworthy for the woman to remain indoors than to live out of doors, but to the man it is less honourable to remain indoors than to attend to outdoor matters. But if any man acts contrary to the natural powers which the God gave him, it is somewhat probable that in violating the order of things he does not escape the gods' notice and pays a penalty for neglecting his own duties or performing his wife's duties. And the queen-bee too," I said, "seems to me to carry out tasks assigned by the God resembling these." "And tell me," she said, "what tasks has the queen-bee, that she is compared to the tasks which I ought to perform?" "It is that she remains," I said, "in the hive and does not suffer the bees to be idle, but sends forth to their work those who are to work outside, and both knows and receives all that each of them brings in, and preserves it until there is need to use it. And when the time for use comes, she apportions to each its due share. And she superintends the combs, the formation of which is being completed within, that they may be formed well and quickly, and she attends to the rising progeny that it may be reared to maturity. And when it is reared and the young ones become fit for work, she sends them to found a colony with one of the young breed as leader." "And shall I too," said my wife, "have to do this?" "You will certainly," I said, "have to remain at home, and send out together those of the servants whose work is out of doors, and you must superintend those whose work is to be done indoors, and you must receive the things which are brought in, and you must apportion whatever of them it is necessary to expend, but must take forethought and care for all that is to be laid by, in order that the provision stored up for the year may not be expended for a month. And when wool is brought in to you, care must be taken that clothes may be made for those who require them. And care must also be taken that the dried provisions may be in good condition for eating. One of the tasks," I added, "which fall to your lot will perhaps seem to be less pleasant, for you must care for all those of the servants who are sick, that they may be tended." "Nay rather," said my wife, "it is assuredly most delightful, if only after being well tended they will feel grateful and be better disposed than before." And I, continued Ischomachus, admiring her answer, said: "Is it then, my wife, on account of some such attentions as these on the part of the leader of the hive also that the bees are so disposed towards her that, when she leaves, not one of the bees thinks that they must stay behind but all follow?" And my wife answered me: "I should be inclined to think that the tasks of the leader concerned you rather than me. For my guardianship and apportionment of the goods at home would seem particularly ridiculous unless you took care that something should be brought in from without." "Again my bringing in supplies," I said, "would seem ridiculous unless there were someone to preserve them when brought in. Do you not see," I continued, "that they who are said to draw water into the bucket with holes in it are pitied because they seem to labour in vain?" "Yes, assuredly," said my wife, "for in truth, if they do this, they are pitiable" "But some other tasks, you know, which fall especially to your lot, my wife," I said, "are pleasant, as when you get a maid who knows nothing of spinning, and make her proficient at it, and she becomes worth twice as much to you; and when you get one who knows nothing of housekeeping and waiting, and succeed in making her proficient and faithful and a good servant, and consider her of inestimable value; and when you have the power to do good to steady servants and such as have been a profit to the household, and have the power to punish any that seems worthless. But it will be the greatest pleasure of all if you are evidently superior to me and make me your servant, and if there is no need for you to fear lest as your age increases you should become less honoured in the household, but if you believe that as you grow older, in proportion as you prove a good partner to me and a good guardian of the house to your children, you will be held in even greater honour in the household. For honours and privileges," I added, "accrue to people more and more, not on account of good looks, but of good deeds in practical life." Such is the conversation, Socrates, which I think I remember holding with her at first

VIII.

Now did you, Ischomachus, I said, observe her to be any the more eager in the work of superintending in consequence of this?

Yes, assuredly, said Ischomachus; and I remember that

she was certainly vexed, and blushed deeply, because when I asked her for one of the articles that had been brought in she could not supply me with it. And I, however, seeing that she was vexed said "Do not be at all discouraged, my wife, because you cannot supply me with that for which I happen to ask you. For this is manifest poverty when one wants a thing not to have it to use, but this want, namely, to seek for a thing and to be unable to find it, is less annoying than not even to seek for it at all, because you know that it does not exist. But now," I said, "you are not to blame for this, but I, for not telling you when I gave things into your charge where each was to be placed, in order that you may know both where you should store it up and whence you should take it. And there is, my wife, nothing either so useful or so seemly among men as order. For, in fact, a chorus is made up of men, but when each performs as chance dictates, a sort of confusion results, and it is unpleasing to look at; but when they perform and sing in an orderly manner then those same actors seem to be both worth seeing and worth hearing. And certainly my wife," I continued, "an army in disorder is all confusion, and a very easy prey to enemies, but to friends it is a thing most unpleasant to behold and most useless—asses, armed soldiers, sutlers, light-armed men, cavalry, waggons, in promiscuous juxtaposition. For how can they march if in this condition they impede one another—the man who is walking him who is running, and the runner him who is stationary, and the waggon the horseman, and the ass the waggon, and the sutler the armed soldier? And if necessity for a battle should arise also, how in this condition can they fight? For those among them who must needs flee from the attacking force are calculated to trample down in their flight the men who are under arms. But an army, when well ordered, is to friends a most glorious sight to behold, but a most grievous one to enemies. For what friend would not rejoice to see a number of armed soldiers marching in order; and who would not admire horsemen riding in companies; and what enemy would not be alarmed at the sight of armed soldiers, horsemen, targeteers, archers, and slingers, well arranged and following their leader in orderly fashion? And, moreover, as they march in order, all, even if there are many thousands, march quietly, just like one man, for into the gap made from time to time those in the rear keep advancing. And again, for what other reason is the trireme, stowed with men, an object of dread to enemies or a worthy spectacle to friends, than that it is a fast sailer? And for what reason are those on board not troublesome to one another, other than that they sit in order and bend forwards and backwards in order, and embark and go ashore in order? But disorder seems to me to be very much as if a farmer were to store together barley and wheat and pulse, and then, when there was need either of dough, or of bread, or of relish, were obliged to pick it out, instead of taking and using what had been carefully separated. And therefore, if you, my wife, do not desire this disorder, but wish to know how to manage to a nicety our possessions, and how to find readily and use such of our possessions as occasion requires, and, if I ask for anything, to gratify me by giving it to me, let us determine the place which each article ought to have, and after putting it therein let us instruct the maid to take it hence and to put it back again in this place; and we shall thus know both what you have and what you have not, for the place itself will miss the absent article and the eye will find out anything requiring attention; and the knowledge where each article is will quickly put it into our hands, so that we shall not be debarred from using it." But I think, Socrates, that I saw the most excellent and accurate arrangement of utensils when I once went on board the great Phœnician vessel in order to look over her. For I saw the largest number of utensils kept separate in the smallest receptacle. For it is, of course, only with the help of a great deal of wooden and woven gear that a ship comes to anchor and puts to sea, and she sails along with the help of much suspended tackle, as it is called, and is armed with many contrivances against hostile vessels, and carries about with the men much armour, and takes for each company of messmates all the utensils which men use in a house, and besides all this she is laden with the cargo which the shipowner carries for profit And all the things I mention, he added, lay in a space not much greater than a well-proportioned room large enough for ten couches. And I noticed that all are placed in a manner in which they do not obstruct one another, nor require someone to hunt for them, nor are they lacking in arrangement or hard to unpack, so as to cause delay when there is need to use something in a hurry. And I found that the captain's mate, who is called the under-pilot of the ship, knew each proper place so well that even if not on the spot he could tell where each article lay, and how many there were, just as well as one who knows his letters could tell how many letters there are in "Socrates," and in what position each is placed. And I saw him, too, said Ischomachus, himself examining during his leisure every single thing which there was need to use on the voyage. And marvelling at his inspection, I asked him, Ischomachus continued, what he was doing. And he said: "I am inspecting the condition of the ship's contents, sir, in case anything happens. to see if anything is either missing or awkwardly placed. For there is no time," he said, "when the God raises a storm at sea, either to hunt for whatever is required or to hand out what is awkwardly placed. For Heaven threatens and punishes the lazy But one must be quite content if only He refrains from destroying those who are not to blame; whereas if He keeps in safety those who do their work thoroughly well, much gratitude," he said, "is due to the gods." I therefore, after noticing this nicety of the equipment. said to my wife that it would be a very stupid thing in us if men on board vessels, even though small, find places for their goods, and though violently tossed nevertheless preserve their order, and though in excess of fear find how to get at what is wanted; and yet if we, who have in the house large separate store-rooms for everything, and our house placed on a firm foundation. shall not find a good and handy place for each article, how can our folly be anything else than great? Now the desirability of having a set of utensils well arranged, and the easiness of finding a place for each of them to store them in the house as suits each, has been shown. And how fair a sight it is when sandals lie in a row, of whatever kind they be; and fair it is to see garments sorted, of whatever kind they be; and how fair to see bedding, and copper vessels, and table gear, and a sight, too, at which not the grave man but the wit would laugh most of all, —for I declare that it appears graceful that even pots should be orderly arranged. And I should say that by this means everything else looks more comely if arranged in order, for each sort looks like a troop of utensils, and the intervening space, too, between these looks well when each kind is kept clear of it; just like a troop of dancers moving in circles is not only itself a fair sight, but the centre of it also looks fair and open. "But as to the question whether my statements are true, we can, my wife," I said, "make trial of them also without any loss and without any great trouble. And further, not even this need discourage us, my wife," I said, "namely, the difficulty of finding one who will both learn the places and remember to put everything in its place. For surely we know that the whole state possesses in all ten thousand times as much as we; but nevertheless, if you bid a servant of any kind purchase and bring you something from the market, not one of them will be at a loss, but everyone will evidently know where he must go to obtain each article. Yet there is no other reason for this," I said, "than that they are kept in the appointed place. But when you are looking for a person, and that sometimes when he is looking for you, you may often give up the search before you find him. And for this, again, there is no other reason than that it has not been arranged where each is to wait." I think, then, that I remember holding some such conversation with her about the arrangement of utensils and their use.

IX.

And what was the result? I said. Did your wife seem

to you, Ischomachus, to give any heed to that which you were anxious to teach her?

Indeed she did, for she made many promises to be careful, and she was evidently greatly delighted, as she had found a means of solution after being in difficulties, and she begged me to arrange things as quickly as possible in the way I mentioned.

Now tell me, Ischomachus, how did you arrange them for her?

Well, I resolved first to show her the capability of the house. For, Socrates, it is not embellished with decorations, but the rooms are built with a view to this simply—that the receptacles may be as convenient as possible for the goods that are to be kept in them, so that they seemed to invite the storage of such goods as were suitable to each one of them. For the bridal chamber, being in a position of security, invited the storage of the most valuable coverlets and utensils, and the dry parts of the rooms the storage of corn, and the cool ones that of wine, while the well-lighted portions invited the presence of all such operations and utensils as require light. And I showed her in succession garnished dwelling rooms for the inmates, cool in summer and warm in winter. And I pointed out to her also that the whole house faces the south, so that it was quite clear that it is sunny in winter and shady in summer. And I showed her also the women's apartments, separated from the men's by a bolted door in order that nothing may be brought out from the former which ought not, and that the servants may not become parents without our knowledge. For good servants become better disposed for having families, but the bad, if they are paired, become readier to do wrong. And when we had surveyed these things, he continued, then we at length set about classifying the moveables in sets. And we began first, he said, by collecting those things which we use at sacrifices. After this we set apart the female attire that is used for festivals, and men's clothing that is used for festivals and war, and bedding in the women's apartments, bedding in the men's women's shoes men s shoes. One division consisted of armour, another of implements for wool-spinning, another of those for bread-making, another of culinary implements, another of those used in bathing, another of those for kneading bread, another of those used at table. And we separated all these into two classes—those that must be used continually, and those suited for festal occasions And we set apart things that are expended month by month, and stored also in a separate place those calculated to last for a year. For thus it is easier seen when they will come to an end. And when we had separated all the moveables into classes, we put them into the several places which suited each. And after this we handed over to the particular persons who used them as many of the utensils as the servants use day by day. such as implements for bread-making, cooking, wool-spinning, or anything else of that sort, pointing out where they must put them; and we charged them to keep them safe. But we handed over to the housekeeper as many as we use for festivals or entertainments, or on occasions which seldom occur, and after pointing out their places and taking an inventory and noting each down, we bade her give each of these to anyone who required it, and remember, when she received back whatever she gave anyone, to restore it again to the exact place whence she took each several article. And we appointed the housekeeper after making an investigation as to who seemed to us to be most temperate with regard to food, wine, sleep, and men's society, and, in addition to this, one who seemed to possess memory and forethought, lest by her neglect she should receive any punishment by our order, and one who seemed, if she did us any favour, to look to be repaid by us with some token of honour. And we began to teach her also to be kindly disposed towards us by allowing her to take part in our joys when we were rejoicing, and if anything painful happened by calling upon her to share this And we trained her to be zealous for the increase of our estate by making her acquainted with our concerns, and by causing her to share our prosperity And we implanted uprightness in her by making the just more honoured than the unjust, and exhibiting them as living in greater luxury and style than the unjust; and we installed her also in the former class. And besides all this, Socrates, he continued, I told my wife that there was no good in all this unless she herself should take care that the arrangement should last in the case of each article. And I taught her that also in well-ordered cities the citizens do not think it sufficient if they draw up good laws, but they in addition to that choose guardians of the law, who act as inspectors, and praise the man who leads a law-abiding life, and if anyone transgress the laws they punish him. I therefore bade my wife consider, he said, that she too was a guardian of the law over those in the house, and also to inspect, whenever she thought fit, the utensils, just as the commandant of a fortress inspects the garrisons, and to try if each is in good condition, just as the senate tries horses and horsemen; and, moreover, to praise and honour like a queen, according to her existing means, him who is deserving, and to censure and punish him who needs such treatment. And in addition to this, I taught her, he said, that she would not be doing right in feeling vexed at my imposing more trouble on her than on the servants with regard to the property, pointing out that servants have only so much to do with their masters' goods as is involved in carrying them, keeping them in order, or guarding them, but none to whom the master does not give permission may use any of them; but all are the master's, for him to make any use he pleases of each. So I tried to make it clear that the care of property also naturally falls to the share of him who derives the greatest profit by its preservation, and the greatest loss by its destruction.

Well, Ischomachus, I said, did your wife grow at all obedient to you after hearing this?

Come, tell me, Socrates, he said, if I was not right in fancying that I was setting her a hard task when I taught her that she must take care of the property? For she said, he continued, that it would have been a harder task if I had ordered her to neglect her own affairs than if she should have to take care of the household goods. For just as it seems to be naturally easier, she said, for the sober-minded woman to care for her own children than to neglect them, so also she said she thought it was a greater pleasure for the sober-minded woman to care for her possessions, which as being her own gladden her, than to neglect them.

X.

And when I heard, said Socrates, that his wife gave him this answer, I said: You most assuredly indicate that your wife's mind is of a masculine character.

And I shall be happy, said Ischomachus, to give you withal other instances of her remarkable high-mindedness, in which, after once receiving my directions, she quickly obeyed.

Of what sort were they? I said. Tell me, as I take much greater delight in hearing of a living woman's good qualities than if Zeuxis were to represent a beautiful woman in a picture and exhibit it to me.

Thereupon Ischomachus said: Well then, Socrates, I once saw her painted with a quantity of white lead so that she might seem to be yet whiter than she was, and with a quantity of alkanet so that she might appear ruddier than in reality, and wearing high shoes that she might seem to be taller than she naturally was. So I said: "Tell me, my wife, in which case you would consider me to be a more lovable joint-owner of property: if I showed you just what I possessed, and neither boasted that I possessed more than I really did, nor concealed any of my possessions; or if I tried to deceive you by saying that I possessed more than I did, and if I showed you spurious money, and plated necklaces, and purple garments that would lose their colour, and said they were genuine." And she at once replied: "Hush! Heaven forbid that you should behave in such a way. For I could not, in that case, love you with all my heart." "Now we have come together, my wife," I said, "with a view to partnership in each other's bodies?" "So men say, at least," she replied. "In which case then again,"

I said, "should I seem to be a more lovable joint-owner of my body, if I endeavoured to present my body to you with every care that it should be both sound and strong, and that I should, therefore, be of a good complexion in your eyes, or if, painting myself with red lead and anointing my eyes with flesh-coloured pigment, I showed myself to you and continued with you, deceiving you and presenting to your sight and touch red lead instead of my own complexion?" "I for my part," she said, "should not be more pleased to touch red lead than your body, nor should I be more pleased to see the hue of a flesh-coloured pigment than yours, nor should I be more pleased to see your eyes anointed than healthy" "Therefore, my wife," Ischomachus said he replied, "consider that I too am not more delighted with the hue either of white lead or of alkanet than with yours, but just as the gods made horses the most pleasant object to horses, and cattle to cattle, and sheep to sheep, so too men think that the most pleasant object is the body in its natural state. And these deceits might, if unquestioned, be in some degree successful in deceiving others, but those who live together must always necessarily be detected if they attempt to deceive one another. For they are either detected rising from bed before making their toilet, or discovered by perspiration, or tested by tears, or owing to bathing espied in their real condition."

What answer, now, in Heaven's name, I said, did she make to this?

None at all, he said, save that in future she never again practised anything of the kind, but endeavoured to show herself in a natural and becoming state. And moreover she used to ask me if I had any advice to give her as to how she might be seen to be beautiful in reality, and not only appear so. And I moreover, Socrates, he continued, used to advise her not to be perpetually seated like a slave, but to endeavour, with the help of the gods, to stand by the loom like a mistress and to give instructions in any method better than another with which she was acquainted, and to learn in any case in which she was acquainted with a worse one, and also to superintend the bread-making, and to stand by the housekeeper too when she was dispensing stores, and go round also and see if each thing was in the place it ought to be. For these acts seemed to me to involve at once superintendence and walking. And I said it was a good thing as an exercise both to moisten and to knead dough and to shake and fold up garments and bedding. And I said that by taking exercise thus she would both eat with greater pleasure and be in better health and be seen to be of a fairer complexion in reality. And a wife's appearance, too, whenever she is contrasted with a servant, if she is more really fair, and more becomingly dressed, becomes attractive, especially whenever willingness to do his pleasure is added, instead of service under compulsion. But women who always remain seated in a dignified fashion expose themselves to be judged by a comparison with those who are gaily dressed and thoroughly deceptive. And now, Socrates, he added, my wife, you may be sure, continues to dress in exact accordance with my instructions, and in such fashion as I am now describing to you.

XI.

Thereupon I said: Now, Ischomachus, I think that I have heard enough of your account of your wife's deeds for a first instalment, and they are certainly calculated to bring you both credit. But in the next place tell me now about your deeds, I said, both in order that you may derive pleasure from recounting for what reasons you are held in esteem, and that I may feel very grateful to you when, if I can do so, I hear and learn to the very end the deeds of the man of good breeding and character.

But most assuredly, Socrates, said Ischomachus, I will recount to you, and that with great pleasure, what I pass my time doing, in order that you may set me right if I seem in any respect to do amiss.

But how, indeed, I said, should I have the right to correct a man of consummate good breeding and character, and that, too, when I am a man who appear to be both a prattler and idle speculator, and am called poor—a charge which seems to be clearly the silliest of all. And I should, in fact, Ischomachus, have been in much despondency on account of this charge had I not lately met the horse of the foreigner Nicias, and seen many gazers following it, and had I not heard some persons holding a long conversation about it. Well now, I went up and asked the groom if the horse had much property. And he stared at me as though I were not even in my right mind to ask such a question, and said: "Why, how can property accrue to a horse?" So I thus recovered my spirits when I heard that it is, it seems, possible for even a poor horse to attain a high character, if he has a soul naturally so inclined. So then, as it is possible for me too to become a man of high character, recount to the end your deeds that I too may endeavour, beginning from to-morrow, to imitate you in whatever I am able to learn on hearing you.

You are joking, Socrates, said Ischomachus, but I will nevertheless recount to you those objects in the pursuit of which I endeavour as far as I can to pass my life. Now inasmuch as I think I have learnt that the gods have made it impossible for men to prosper without they both know what things they ought to do, and take care that these may be fulfilled, and that they grant happiness to some if they are prudent and careful, and not to others, I thereupon begin by serving the gods in order that I, their suppliant, may be permitted to attain both health and strength of body, and honour in civic life, and popularity among friends, and in war honourable escape, and an increase of wealth by honourable means.

And I, on hearing this, replied: Why, do you really care, Ischomachus, to grow rich, and through having much property to have much trouble in taking care of it?

Most certainly, said Ischomachus, I do care about this property concerning which you ask; for it seems to me, Socrates, a pleasant thing both to worship the gods with magnificence and to aid one's friends if they stand in need of anything, and that the state should not be in any degree, as far as depends on me, unfurnished with money

Well really, Ischomachus, I said, the actions which you mention are honourable, and such as belong to a highly influential man. For how can it be otherwise when there are many men who cannot live without standing in need of others' help, and many are content if they can provide what is sufficient for themselves? And how, indeed, can we help calling those who are able not only to manage their own household, but also to leave a surplus wherewith to embellish the city and also to relieve their friends, men of substance and power? No doubt many of us, I said, can extol such men; but tell me, Ischomachus (with which matters, indeed, you began), how you care for your health, how for your bodily strength, and how it is possible for you to escape honourably even from war. And as to the money making, I said, it will suffice to hear of that after all this.

But all these things, in my opinion at least, Socrates, said Ischomachus, are consequent one upon another. For when a man has enough to eat, his health seems to me more likely to be preserved if he works hard, and by hard work his strength seems more likely to increase, and if he practises military exercises there is more likelihood of his escaping with greater honour, and, if he takes due care and does not relax into idleness, of his estate increasing.

Now I follow you, Ischomachus, I said so far: that you say that a man who works hard and is provident and exercises himself attains greater prosperity; but I should gladly be informed, I said, on these points: what sort of work you practise with a view to good health and strength, and how you exercise yourself in military matters, and how you provide for securing a surplus so as to aid friends and also to strengthen the city.

Well then, Socrates, said Ischomachus, I have been in the habit of rising from bed at a time when, if I happened to want to see anyone, I should find him still at home. And if I have to do any business in the city, while I am carrying this on I make it serve as a walk; but if there is nothing of importance in the city, my servant leads my horse in advance of me into the country, and I make the journey into the country serve as a walk better perhaps than if, Socrates, I were to walk about in the arcade. And when I get into the country, if men who are either planting or working on fallow land or sowing or gathering in the harvest come under my notice, I watch how each of these operations is being performed and change the method if I know of any better than the present one. And after this I generally mount my horse and practise riding as similar to the riding required in war as I can, turning aside neither from slanting nor from steep ground, nor from ditch, nor canal. However I take care as far as possible not to lame my horse while he is doing so. And when this is finished my servant leads the horse home after letting him have a roll, at the same time bringing to town from the country anything we require. And I go home sometimes at a walking pace, sometimes running, and scrape myself clean. And then, Socrates, I take a morning meal just sufficient to allow me to pass the day without either an empty or an overladen stomach.

In good truth, Ischomachus, I said, you do all this just in the manner that pleases me For at the same time to carry on arrangements conducive both to health and strength at once, and military exercises, and attention to money making—all this seems to me to be admirable. And indeed you furnish abundant proof that you duly attend to each of these objects, for we see you with the help of the gods for the most part both hale and strong, and we know that you are reckoned among the best riders and most wealthy men.

Now though I thus act, Socrates, he said, I am sorely slandered by many; and you were perhaps thinking that I should say that I have been styled a man of good breeding and character by many.

True; but I was about to ask this also, Ischomachus, I said, whether you pay any attention to this object too; namely, that you may be able to render and receive an account of conduct, if it ever be necessary to render such to anyone.

Why, do I not seem to you, Socrates, to be continually engaged in this very thing, namely, in saying in my own defence that I do wrong to no man, and that I do good as far as lies in my power to many? And do I not seem to you to be engaged in bringing charges against men, when I learn that many commit injustice in private life and some too against the state, while they do good to none?

Now show me this one thing more, Ischomachus, I said, whether you are engaged also in expounding such sentiments.

Well, Socrates, he said, on no occasion do I cease from my occupation of speaking For either when I hear one of the servants bringing a charge or making a defence I endeavour to prove him wrong, or I blame someone before his friends or praise him, or I try to reconcile some of my acquaintances, endeavouring to teach them how much better it is for them to be friends rather than enemies. We censure a man when we are present with a general, or we make a defence on his behalf if he is unjustly the subject of an accusation, or we bring charges before one another if anyone is unjustly honoured. And often, too, when we consult together we praise those objects which we desire to accomplish, and find fault with those which we do not wish to accomplish. And often before now, Socrates, he added, I was even distinctly put on my trial as to what punishment I must suffer or what fine I must pay.

By whom, Ischomachus? I said. For this was really unknown to me.

By my wife, he said.

And how then, I said, do you plead your cause?

Whenever it is to my advantage to speak the truth, very fairly well; but when I need a lie, Socrates, I assuredly cannot make the weaker argument the stronger.

And I said: That is perhaps because, Ischomachus, you cannot make the lie true.

XII.

But now, Ischomachus, I said, am I detaining you when you are already anxious to take your leave?

Assuredly not, Socrates, he said; for I should not leave before the market is quite over.

Of course not, I said, for you are taking good care not to forfeit being called by the surname of "man of good breeding and character." For now, though many matters perhaps require your attention, since you made an appointment with the strangers, you are awaiting them, in order that you may not break your engagement

Yet indeed, Socrates, said Ischomachus, not even those matters of which you speak are being neglected by me, for I have bailiffs in the country

But Ischomachus, I said, when you require a balilff, after getting to know if there is a man qualified as a bailiff to be had, whether do you attempt to purchase this man (just as when you require a carpenter, after getting to know, as I am sure you do, if you can see anywhere one qualified as a carpenter, you endeavour to purchase that man) or do you yourself rear your bailiffs?

Assuredly I endeavour, Socrates, he said, to rear them myself For indeed what need at all is there for the man who is to be competent, whenever I am away, to take charge in my place, to know anything else than just what I know? For if I am able to manage my business, I could, I suppose, teach another too what I myself know.

Then first it will be necessary, I said, that he should have a kindly disposition to you and yours, if he is to be competent when on the spot instead of you For without a kindly disposition what advantage accrues even from knowledge of any possible kind whatever on a bailiff's part?

None assuredly, said Ischomachus, and in fact a kindly disposition towards me and mine is the first thing in which I endeavour to train them.

And how, in Heaven's name, I said, do you teach anyone you please to be kindly disposed to you and yours?

By treating them kindly, assuredly, said Ischomachus, whenever the gods grant us abundance of any blessing.

Do you then mean this, I said, that those who have the enjoyment of your blessings become well disposed towards you and wish to do you a good turn?

Yes, Socrates: for I perceive that this is the best means of producing a kindly disposition.

And then if he becomes kindly disposed towards you, Ischomachus, I said, will he on this account be competent to act as bailiff? Do you not see that even though all men are, generally speaking, kindly disposed towards themselves, there are many of them who are unwilling to take care that they may have those blessings which they wish to have?

But in good truth, said Ischomachus, whenever I want to appoint men of that sort bailiffs I teach them also to be careful.

In Heaven's name, how? I said. For I thought that this was in fact a thing that could not be taught; namely, to make a man careful

No more it is possible, Socrates, he said, to teach all without exception to be careful.

What sort of men then can you teach? I said. By all means point out these clearly to me.

In the first place, Socrates, he said, you would not be able to make those who are intemperate in the use of wine careful; for drunkenness produces forgetfulness of everything that needs doing.

Then are those only who are intemperate in this matter unable to be careful, I said, or are there some others also?

Yes, assuredly, said Ischomachus; those too who are intemperate in the use of sleep For the man who is asleep would be able neither himself to do what is needful nor to make others attentive

How now? I said Shall we count these again alone incapable of being taught this carefulness, or some others also in addition to these?

Those, indeed, too, said Ischomachus, who are desperately involved in matters of love, are incapable of being taught to care for anything else in preference to that; for it is not easy to find any more pleasant hope and employment than attention to love affairs; nor, indeed, whenever business arises, is it easy to find a severer punishment than to be kept away from the beloved objects. I therefore give up even trying to appoint stewards any of those also whomsoever I observe to be men of this sort.

Well then, I said, are those again who are deeply attached to money-making also incapable of being trained to the superintendence of rustic operations?

Assuredly not, said Ischomachus; they are not in the least so, but are in fact quite easily brought up to the superintendence of these affairs; for nothing else is needed than merely to show them that the superintendence is a profitable matter.

And how do you instruct the rest, I said, to become attentive to the matters that you wish, if they are both temperate in such respects as you require and indifferently disposed with regard to money-making?

By quite a simple method, Socrates, he said. For whenever I see them careful, I endeavour both to praise and honour them; but whenever I see them careless, I endeavour both to say and do such things as will sting them to the quick

Come, Ischomachus, I said, and, digressing from the argument about those who are trained to this superintendence, demonstrate to me this also concerning the training, if it is possible for a man who is himself careless to make others careful.

Assuredly not said Ischomachus, no more than it is possible for one who is himself illiterate to make others scholars For it is difficult, when the teacher sets a bad example in anything, to learn to do this well; and so, when the master sets an example of carelessness it is difficult for a servant to become careful And, to put the matter briefly, I do not think that I have observed a bad master's servants to be good. I have, however, before this noticed those of a good master to be bad but not, however, without suffering for it But he who wishes to make men careful must be able to both supervise and examine, and willing to bestow a reward on him who is the cause of what is accomplished well, and without hesitation in inflicting on the careless the penalty he deserves And the answer which it is said the foreigner gave, said Ischomachus, seems to me to be well put. For when the king, after he had met with a good horse, wished to fatten him as soon as possible, and asked one of those who seemed to be skilled with regard to horses what would most quickly fatten a horse, it is said that he replied, "His master's eye." So, too, Socrates, he added, the master's eye seems to me to be most efficient in accomplishing all other honourable and good objects.

XIII.

But when you succeed in impressing ever so firmly on a man, I said, that he must take care of whatever you wish, will such a man be forthwith competent to act as bailiff, or will something else, too, have to be learnt by him, if he is to be a competent bailiff?

Yes, assuredly, said Ischomachus, it indeed still remains for him to know both what is to be done, and when, and how. Otherwise, what greater advantage would there be in a bailiff without this knowledge, than in a physician who attended a patient, coming both early and late, but was ignorant of what it was for the benefit of his patient to do?

But now, if he learns, too, how the work is to be done, I said, will he still need anything further, or will this man now be your perfect bailiff?

Well, I think, he said, that he ought to learn to govern the workers

Do you, then, I said, train the bailiffs to be competent to govern, too?

I certainly try, at all events, said Ischomachus.

And how now, in Heaven's name, I said, do you train them to be fit to govern men?

Quite easily, Socrates, he said, so that perhaps you would even laugh if you were to hear.

Indeed, the matter certainly does not deserve ridicule, Ischomachus, I said. For it is surely evident that he who can make others fit to govern men can also teach them to become fitted to be masters of men; and whoever can fit them to be masters can also make them fit to be kings. So that he who can do this seems to me to deserve not ridicule, but great praise.

Well now, Socrates, he said, all other living beings learn obedience from these things, namely, from being punished whenever they attempt to be disobedient, and from being treated well whenever they perform their services readily.

Colts, at all events, learn to submit to horsebreakers through something pleasant happening to them whenever they are obedient, and by getting into trouble when they are disobedient, until they do their horsebreaker service according to his will. And puppies, too, though they are far inferior to men, both in their intelligence and in their power of expression, nevertheless learn in the same way both to run round and round, and to turn somersets, and many other tricks For whenever they are obedient they receive something that they want, but whenever they are careless they are punished. And it is possible to make men more obedient even by a word, but with slaves the training which seems to be fit for beasts is also very conducive towards teaching them to be obedient, for were you to gratify their stomach with respect to its desires, you would succeed in getting much from them. But the ambitious natures are spurred on by praise too. For some natures are no less hungry for praise than others are for food and drink. These methods, then, by employing which myself I expect to find men more obedient, I teach to all those whom I wish to appoint bailiffs, and in these ways I help them; for I do not make all the clothing and shoes which I must provide for the workpeople of the same qualtity, but some inferior and some better, in order that it may be possible to honour the more efficient workman with the better articles and to give the inferior man those of less value. For discouragement certainly seems to me, Socrates, he said, to arise among the good whenever they see that, though the work is accomplished by their means, those who will neither labour nor incur danger, whenever that is necessary, meet with the same treatment as themselves. Therefore I myself do not in any way whatever think it right that the better men should meet with treatment equal to that of the worse, and I also praise the bailiffs when I know that they have distributed the best things to the most deserving, but if I see anyone preferred through flattery or such other improper gratification, I do not disregard it, but I reprimand him and try to teach him, Socrates, that he does not do this even to his own interest.

XIV.

But when your man, Ischomachus, I said, at length becomes competent to govern too, so as to make them obedient, do you consider this man a perfect bailiff, or does he who possesses the qualifications which you have mentioned yet need anything further?

Yes, assuredly, said Ischomachus; he needs to keep his hands off his master's property and not to steal. For if he who has the management of the produce were to dare to make away with it to such an extent as not to allow it to yield a profit on the working expenses, what would be the use of working a farm under this man's superintendence?

Do you, then, undertake, I said, to teach this honesty also?

Most certainly, said Ischomachus. But I do not, for all that, find that all accept this teaching readily. And yet I endeavour, he said, by taking some enactments from Draco's laws, and some also from those of Solon, to lead my servants to honesty. For it seems to me, he said, that these men too made many of their laws with a view to teaching honesty of this sort. For it has been enacted that if anyone is taken in the act, he is punished for theft, and imprisoned, and that those guilty of assault are put to death. It is clear, then, he said, that they enacted them with a desire to make wrongful gain unprofitable to the dishonest. I, therefore, he continued adopting some of these, and also other enactments from the laws of kings, endeavour to render the servants honest in respect to the property they manage. For, while former laws are only a punishment to transgressors, the laws of kings not only punish the dishonest, but also benefit the honest; so that many, seeing that the honest become richer than the dishonest, and being greedy of gain, take good care to continue to avoid dishonesty. But I remove even from intercourse with myself, he said, as being incorrigible gain-getters, all those whom I perceive, though they are treated well, nevertheless to be still endeavouring to be dishonest. But I treat just like men already free all those, again, whom I observe to be induced to be honest, not only by the fact of their being gainers on account of their honesty, but also by their desire of being praised by me; and I not only enrich them, but also honour them as men of good breeding and character For in this respect, Socrates, he said, an ambitious man seems to me to differ from a covetous man, namely, in being willing for the sake of praise and honour both to labour when necessary, and to incur danger, and to refrain from dishonest gains.

XV.

Now, however, after you have implanted in a man the wish that you may have prosperity, and have implanted in this same man the disposition to take care that this may be realized to you; and, moreover, in addition to this, have gained for him a knowledge how each of the farming operations should be done to be turned to greater profit; and, in addition to this, have made him competent to govern; and when, besides all this, he is delighted at exhibiting you the timely fruits of the earth in as large quantities as possible, just in the same degree as you would be at exhibiting them to yourself; I will no longer ask, concerning this man, if such an one yet needs something further; for I am altogether of the opinion that such a man would already be very valuable as a bailiff. However, Ischomachus, I said, do not neglect that part of our subject which has been most cursorily passed over by us.

Which is that? said Ischomachus

You said, you know, I answered, that it was a very great matter to learn how one ought to perform each operation; and you said that otherwise no profit arose even from supervision, unless one knew what one ought to do and how one ought to do it

So upon this Ischomachus said · Do you now bid me, Socrates, teach you the art itself of agriculture?

Yes; for this, I said, is apparently the art that makes those who understand it rich, and makes such as do not understand it pass their life in want though they toil much.

Now, therefore, Socrates, he said, you shall hear of the

kindliness of this art. For how can it be other than a noble thing that, being most profitable and most pleasant to work at, and most honourable and agreeable to both gods and men, it should yet be, in addition to this, also most easy to learn. And, you know, we call those beasts noble also which, while they are comely and great and serviceable, are gentle towards mankind.

Now, as to these matters, Ischomachus, I said, I think that I have learnt thoroughly enough how you described by what method one must instruct the bailiff; for I think I learnt how you said you make him well disposed towards yourself, and how you make him careful, and fit to govern, and honest. But, with regard to what you said as to how he who is to give due attention to agriculture must learn both what he ought to do and how and when he ought to perform each operation, we seem to me, I said, to have passed over these questions somewhat too cursorily in our conversation; just as if you were to say that he who is to be able to write what is being dictated, and to read what has been written, must know his letters. For, after hearing this, I should have heard, indeed, that I must know my letters, but I should not, I fancy, know my letters any better for being aware of this. And so now, too, I am easily convinced that he who is to give due attention to it must understand agriculture, yet I do not know any better how to farm for being aware of this. But, if I were to resolve at this very moment to be a farmer, I think I should be like the physician who goes round and visits his patients but does not know at all what is for his patients' good. So, in order that I may not be such an one, I said, teach me the actual operations of agriculture.

Well but, Socrates, he said, though in the case of the other arts people must be bored to death with learning before the pupil performs work worth his maintenance, agriculture is not in the same way also irksome to learn, but, were you to see them performing some operations and to hear about others, you would at once understand, so as, if you wished, even to teach another. And I think, too, he added, that, without being at all aware of the fact, you know many points of this art. For of course the other artisans make some secret of the most important points of the arts which each plies, while among farm labourers the best planter would be specially delighted if anyone were to watch him, and likewise the best sower; and whatever piece of good work you asked about, he would not hide from you how he did any single thing. Thus, too, Socrates, is agriculture wont, he said, to make most noble in their dispositions those who have to do with it.

Certainly, I said, the preamble is excellent. and not such as to make one, after hearing it, give up his question; but, inasmuch as it is easy to learn, do you for that reason all the more describe the art in detail to me. For it is no disgrace to you to teach easy subjects, but much more disgraceful for me not to know them, especially if they happen to be profitable.

XVI.

In the first place then, Socrates, he said, I want to shew you this—that what is said to be the most intricate point of agriculture in theory by those who describe it most accurately, but practise it very little. is not a difficult one. For they say that he who is to farm properly ought first to know the nature of the soil

Yes, and rightly, I replied, do they say this. For, if a man did not know what the soil could produce, neither would he know, I fancy, what he ought to sow, nor what he ought to plant.

Well then, said Ischomachus, it is possible, even in the case of another man's ground, to learn both what it can produce and what it cannot, by noticing the crops and the trees. Yet. after a man has learnt that, there is no longer any use in contending with Providence. For it is by sowing and planting, not so much that which he wanted as that which the ground readily produced and supported, that a man would obtain the necessaries of life But if, indeed. through idleness on the part of the occupiers, it is unable to exhibit its own capacity, it is also often possible to gain truer knowledge about it from a neighbouring plot than from enquiries of a neighbouring proprietor. And even though it lies waste, it nevertheless exhibits its own nature For the ground whose wild products are excellent can, when cared for, bring its cultivated products also to excellence. In fact, even those who are quite unskilled in agriculture can nevertheless thus discern a soil's nature.

Well, Ischomachus, I said, I think I am by this time sufficiently confident on this point—that I ought not to refrain from agriculture for fear of not knowing the soil's nature. For in fact, he continued, I am reminded of what the fishermen do—how, though their work is on the sea, and though they neither stop the vessel in order to observe nor progress leisurely, yet all the time, as they scud past the fields, they do not, for all that, whenever they see the crops on the land, hesitate to declare concerning the soil what sort is good and what sort bad, but find fault with the one and praise the other. And, indeed, I notice that they generally give their opinion as to the good soil in the same manner as those well skilled in agriculture.

From what point do you then wish me, Socrates, he said, to begin to bring agriculture to your recollection? For I know that I shall in you be addressing one who knows to a very great extent how one ought to farm.

I think, Ischomachus, I said, that I should like first to learn this (for it especially concerns a man who is a philosopher)—how I should cultivate land to obtain, if I wished, most barley and most wheat.

Well, you know this, that you must prepare fallow land for sowing?

Yes, I know that, I said.

Suppose, then, we were to begin, he said, to plough the land in winter?

But it would be mud, I said.

Then does it seem well to you to plough in summer?

The ground, I said, will be hard to break with the team.

It seems, he said, that a beginning ought to be made in this task in spring.

Yes, for it is likely that the ground, when broken at that season, crumbles most.

And that even the grass, Socrates, if turned up, he said, at that season, already furnishes manure for the ground, not having yet shed its seed so as to spring up again. For I suppose, of course, that you moreover know this too, that, if newly ploughed land is to be of good quality, it must be both clear of undergrowth and baked as much as possible in the sun.

I think that this too, I said, must be exactly so.

Then, do you think that this would be better achieved in any other way than if one were to turn over the ground as often as possible in summer?

I know indeed for a certainty, I said, that in no way would the undergrowth lie more on the surface or be more dried up and the ground be more baked by the sun, than if one were to break it up in midsummer and at mid-day with the team.

But if men should make fallow land by digging it up, he said, is it not evident that these too must separate the soil and the undergrowth?

They must, I said, both strew the undergrowth on the surface that it may be dried, and turn the ground over that the unexposed part of it may be baked.

XVII.

As to the newly ploughed land, Socrates, he said, you see that we both think alike.

Yes, we do, I said.

As to sowing, however, have you, Socrates, he said, any other opinion than to sow at that season of which all former generations made trial, and have found it to be best, as do all those who now try it? For, after the autumn season has come, all men, I suppose, look up to the God for the time when, by sending rain upon the earth, He will give them an opportunity of sowing

Yes, all men have certainly resolved too, Ischomachus, I said, not willingly to sow in a dry soil; those of them who sowed before they were ordered by the God having evidently contended with grievous losses.

Well, all of us men, said Ischomachus, admit the truth of that.

Yes, for it comes to pass in this way, I said, that we are

of one mind with regard to what the God teaches us. For instance, all think it is better to wear thick clothing in the winter, if they can: and all, without exception, think well to burn a fire, if they have wood.

But in this matter, said Ischomachus, many differ forthwith about the sowing, Socrates, as to whether the early or that in mid-season, or the latest, is best.

But the God, I said, does not govern the year according to a fixed rule, but sometimes in a manner most favourable to the early sowing, and sometimes to that in mid-season, and sometimes to the latest.

Whether do you think it, then, Socrates, to be better to select and adopt one of these seed-times, both if a man sows much seed and if he sows little, or to begin from the earliest and go on sowing till the latest?

And I said It seems to me, Ischomachus, that it is best to take part in the whole seed-time. For I think that it is much better to obtain always sufficient corn than a great deal in one season and not even enough in another.

And in this matter you are, in fact, Socrates, he said, in agreement with me, the learner with the teacher, and that, too, though you deliver your opinion before me.

Well now, I said, is any intricate art involved in scattering the seed?

By all means, Socrates, he said, let us consider this point too Now you too, I suppose, know that the seed must be cast from the hand? he added.

Yes, for I have even seen it done, I said.

And some can scatter it evenly, while others cannot.

Then this matter, I said, forthwith requires attention, just as with those who play the lyre the hand does, that it may be able to do the mind's bidding.

Exactly so, he said; and then, if the soil be some lighter, some richer? he added.

What is it, I said, that you mean? Do you ask whether I would sow the lighter soil as if weaker, and the richer as if stronger?

I do mean this, he said, and I ask you whether you would allot the same quantity of seed to each kind of land, or to which you would allot more.

I think it right, I said, to pour in more water to the stronger wine; and to lay a heavier burden, if there is need to carry anything, on the stronger man; and, if any children had to be reared, I should assign to the richer persons the larger number to rear. But do you instruct me on this point, I said, whether the weak soil becomes stronger if one cast more grain on it, as is the case with beasts of burden

And Ischomachus laughed and said: Now you are joking, Socrates Yet you may rest assured, he added, that if, after casting the seed on the soil, you then, after the sprouting of the blade from the seed at the period when the earth is obtaining much nourishment from the fall of rain, plough it in again, this serves as nourishment for the soil, and strength accrues to it, just as from manure. If, however, you allow the soil all the time to go on rearing the seed to maturity, it is difficult for the weak soil to bring much fruit to perfection. And it is difficult, too, for a weak sow to rear a large number of fine porkers.

Do you mean, Ischomachus, that one should cast the seed more sparingly on the weaker soil?

Yes, assuredly, Socrates, he said; and indeed you admit this by saying that you think it right to allot less burdens to all the weaker agents.

And now as to the hoers, Ischomachus, I said, for what purpose do you set them to work on the corn?

You are of course aware, he said, that in winter there is much water about.

Certainly I am, I replied.

Therefore let us suppose that some part of the corn was covered up by it, and a coat of mud spread over, and that some of the roots were laid bare by a flood. And often, you know, undergrowth too shoots up along with the corn on account of the rains, and causes it to be choked.

It is likely, I said, that all these things would happen

Then the corn seems to you, he said, at that time to require forthwith some assistance?

Most certainly, I replied.

By what operation, then, does it seem to you that they would assist that which was deluged with mud?

By lifting up the soil, I said.

And how, he said, would they assist that which had been bared at the root?

By heaping the soil about it again, I said.

Now, how if undergrowth choke it, he said, shooting up together with the corn, and taking away its nourishment from the corn, just as the drones, useless as they are, take away from the bees whatever nourishment they lay up in store after toiling for it?

It would assuredly, I said, be necessary to root up the undergrowth, just as it is to exclude the drones from the hives.

Do we not therefore seem, he said, rightly to set the hoers to work?

Certainly. Now I am thinking, I said, Ischomachus, what a good thing it is to introduce your illustrations happily. For you made me quite angry with the undergrowth by mentioning the drones, much more so than when you were speaking simply of the undergrowth.

XVIII.

To pass on, I said, it is probable that after this we should then reap. So instruct me on this subject too, if you have any information to give.

I will, unless you should be found, he said, to have the same knowledge as I on this subject also. Now you know it is necessary to cut the corn.

And how can I fail to know that? I said.

Whether, then, do you cut it, he said, standing on the side whence the wind is blowing, or facing the wind?

Not facing the wind, for my part, I said; for I think that reaping against stalks and bearded ears is disagreeable both to the eyes and the hands.

And again, would you, he said, cut it off at the top, or cut it close to the ground?

If the stalk of the corn were short, I said, I should cut it from below, that the straw might be more serviceable; but, if it were tall, I think I should do right in cutting it in the middle, in order that neither the threshers nor the winnowers might toil at unnecessary work on that of which they have no need. And I consider that the portion left in the ground would, if burnt, help to benefit the soil, and also, if thrown on for manure, would help to increase the manure.

You see, Socrates, he said, that you are convicted in the very act of knowing just what I know about harvesting too.

It seems that I am, I said, and I want to see if I know how to thresh also

Well, he said, you know this, that they tread out the corn by means of a beast of burden.

How can I help knowing it? I said. Also, that all alike are called beasts of burden: oxen, mules, and horses.

Now do you think that these beasts know nothing more than this, namely, how to trample upon the corn when they are driven?

For what else, I said, should beasts of burden know?

But by what means, Socrates, he said, do they know this—how they shall tread on that which requires it, and how the threshing shall be kept level?

It is evident, I said, that they know this by means of those who superintend the threshing. For by turning and throwing under the animals' feet what is from time to time untrodden they would evidently keep the threshing floor most level, and get the work done most quickly.

Now you are, he said, in no respect inferior to me in your knowledge of this.

Therefore, Ischomachus, I said, after this we will next separate the chaff from the grain by winnowing.

And now tell me, Socrates, said Ischomachus, do you know that, if you begin from the side of the threshing floor next to the wind, your husks will be carried over the whole threshing floor?

Yes, for it must be so, I said.

Then it is probable, he said, that they would fall even upon the corn.

Yes, for it is a great matter, I said, that the husks should be carried beyond the corn to the vacant part of the threshing floor.

And suppose, he said, that a man were to winnow beginning on the lee-side?

It is evident, I said, that the husks will immediately fall into the receptacle meant for them.

And after you have separated the grain from the chaff, he said, as far as the middle of the threshing floor, whether will you, while the corn lies spread out, at once winnow the remaining grain, or after thrusting the winnowed corn together towards the edge into as narrow a space as possible?

Assuredly, I said, after thrusting together the winnowed corn, in order that my husks may be carried across to the vacant part of the threshing floor, and that it may not be necessary to winnow the same grain twice.

Well then, Socrates, he said, you would even be able to teach another how corn may be most quickly winnowed.

Then I knew these things, I said, without being aware of the fact. And I have for some time been thinking whether I know perhaps how to work in gold, and to play the flute, and to paint from life, without being aware of it. For no one taught me either these things or how to farm, and I see men plying the other arts, too, just in the same way as they farm.

Therefore, said Ischomachus, I told you just now that in this respect, too, agriculture was a most noble art, namely, that it was also very easy to learn.

Well now, Ischomachus, I said, I know that. In fact, though I knew about sowing, I knew it, indeed, without being aware of the fact.

XIX.

Now, does the planting of trees, I said, also belong to the art of agriculture?

Yes, indeed it does, said Ischomachus.

How then should I know about sowing, I said, and not know about planting?

Why, do you not know? said Ischomachus.

How should I? I said; for I know neither in what sort of soil it is necessary to plant, nor to what depth to dig a hole for the sapling, nor of what width, nor of what length it is necessary that the sapling should be when put in, nor in what position in the soil the sapling would grow best.

Come then, said Ischomachus, learn whatever you do not know. Now I am sure, he continued, that you have seen what sort of holes they dig for the saplings.

Yes, I have, and very often, I said.

Did you ever see one of them deeper than three feet?

Assuredly I never saw one, I said, deeper than two feet and a half.

Well, as to the width, did you ever see one more than three feet?

Assuredly never above two feet, I said.

Come then, he said, answer me this, too, did you ever see one less than a foot in depth?

Assuredly, I said, I never saw one less than a foot and a half. For the saplings would, in fact, be rooted up when dug about, I said, if they had been planted so much too near the surface.

Then, Socrates, you know this well enough, he said, that they dig the hole neither deeper than two feet and a half nor shallower than one foot and a half.

For this could not but be noticed, I said, since it is so very evident.

Well now, he said, do you know a drier soil and a moister one when you see them?

That around Lycabettus, and such as that, I said, seems to me to be dry at any rate; and that in the marsh of Phalerum, and such as that, seems to be moist.

Whether then would you, he said, dig a deep hole for the sapling in the dry soil or in the moist?

In the dry soil, assuredly, I said; for, were you to dig a deep one in the moist soil, you would find water, and you could not, after that, plant in water.

You seem to me, he said, to say well. Then, did you ever notice at what season it is necessary to put the saplings in each sort of soil, after the holes have been dug?

Certainly, I said.

If, then, you wished them to grow as quickly as possible, whether do you think that the sprout from the cutting, after you put some well-prepared earth under it, would strike more quickly through the soft soil, or through the unbroken soil into the hard ground?

It is evident, I said, that it would sprout more quickly through the well-prepared than through the unbroken soil.

Then soil would have to be put under the sapling.

How can it be otherwise ? I said.

Whether do you think that it would take root better if you set the whole cutting upright, looking towards the sky, or would you lay it partly slantwise under the soil that had been cast upon it, so that it would lie just like a reversed gamma ?

In the latter way, assuredly; for the buds would be to a greater extent under the ground, and I notice the saplings sprouting from the buds above ground, too, and I therefore expect that the buds under the ground do the same. And if many sprouts grew under the ground, I expect that the sapling would sprout quickly and be hardy.

About these matters too, then, he said, you happen to have the same knowledge as I have. And would you merely, he added, heap up the soil, or would you also press it down quite tightly around the sapling ?

I would assuredly press it down, I said. For, if it had not been pressed down, I am sure that the unpressed earth would be turned by the rain into mud, and would be dried to the bottom by the sun; so that there would be a danger of the sapling being rotted by the rain owing to moisture, and of its being dried up owing to drought or the soil's porousness, the roots becoming heated.

Then about the planting of vines, too, Socrates, he said, you happen to have in all respects the same knowledge as I have.

Must we plant a fig-tree, too, in this way ? I said.

I suppose so, said Ischomachus, and all the other fruit-trees also For of which of the means that are successful in the planting of the vine would you disapprove in respect to the other kinds of planting ?

And how, Ischomachus, I said, shall we plant the olive ?

In this, too, you are making trial of me, he said, for you know perfectly well. For of course you notice that a deeper hole is dug for the olive; and, indeed, it is dug generally by the roadsides; and you observe that there are stems to all the young plants; and you observe that clay lies on all the tops of the saplings, and that the upper parts of all the plants is covered up.

I observe all these points, I said.

And when you do observe them, he said, which of them do you not understand? Is it, Socrates, he continued, that you do not know how you would place the potsherd on the clay at the top?

There is, assuredly, nothing in what you told me, I said, which I do not understand, Ischomachus; but I am again thinking why it was that, when just now you were asking me generally if I knew how to plant, I said I did not. For I did not think that I should be able to say anything at all as to the way in which one ought to plant; but, when you undertook to ask me each point separately, I give you in my answers, as you say, that very information which you, who are called a skilful farmer, possess. Is questioning, then, Ischomachus, I said, a means of teaching? For now at last I understand, I continued, how you asked each question, for, leading me on through things which I understand, by pointing out things similar to these, you make me believe, I suppose, that I understand those things too which I thought I did not understand.

Could I then, said Ischomachus, by asking you about money too, whether it was good or not, persuade you that you know how to test the good and the base coins? And by asking you about flute-players, could I make you believe that you know how to play the flute? and so by asking you about painters, and about all other such?

Perhaps you could, I said, since you make me believe that I was an adept at farming, although I know that no one ever taught me this art

This is impossible, Socrates, he said; but I was telling you a little while ago, too, that agriculture is so kindly and gracious an art as to make those who either see it or hear about it proficient in it at once. And in many cases, he said, it even itself affords information as to how a man would practise it to the greatest advantage. For instance, a vine, by climbing up the trees whenever it has any tree near, teaches us to prop it up; and, by spreading out its leaves while its bunches of grapes are yet tender, it teaches us to provide shade for the parts exposed to the sun at that time of year; but, by shedding its leaves when it is the season for the clusters to be forthwith sweetened by the sun, it teaches us to strip it and to cause its fruit to ripen; and, owing to its productiveness, it exhibits some ripe bunches of grapes, while it still bears others less ripe, teaching us to gather from it, just as they gather figs, the fruit which successively swells to ripeness.

XX

After that I said: How then is it, Ischomachus, if it be true both that the details of agriculture are so easy to learn, and that all know equally well what they ought to do, that all do not also fare alike, but that some of them live in opulence and have a surplus, while others cannot provide for themselves even the necessaries of life, but run into debt besides?

Well, I will tell you, Socrates, said Ischomachus. Now it is not the knowledge or the ignorance of the farmers that causes some to be well off and others to be in want; nor would you, he continued, hear a report spreading after this fashion: that the estate has been brought to utter ruin because the sower did not sow evenly, or because he did not plant the rows straight, or because a man, not knowing that the land in question was productive of vines, planted them in an unproductive soil, or because a man did not know that it is a good thing to prepare fallow land for sowing, or because a man did not know how good it is to mix manure with the soil; but one may hear much more frequently: the man is not getting any corn from his field, for he does not take care that it may be sown for him or that manure may be put in it; and, the man has no wine, for he does not take care to plant vines, or that those which he has may bear him fruit; and, the man has no olive-oil or figs, for he does not take care or set to work, so that he may have them. Such are the points, Socrates, he said, by differing from one another on which the farmers fare also much more differently than those who seem to have discovered some clever device for doing their work. And generals who do not differ from one another in mental power, but who evidently differ in diligence, with regard to some of a general's duties, are some better generals and others worse. For some of the leaders do, and others do not do, those things which the generals all know how to do, and most of the private soldiers too All know this, for instance, that it is better for men, when marching through an enemy's territory, to march drawn up in such a manner that they would fight, if it were necessary, to the greatest advantage Being therefore possessed of this knowledge, some act on it, and others do not. All know that it is better to station companies of sentinels both day and night before the camp. And some take care with regard to this too, that it may be so, and others take no care. And again it is very hard to find anyone who does not know that, whenever they go through a narrow pass in any place, it is better to seize the advantageous positions beforehand than not to do so. And, with regard to this too, some take care to do so and others do not. And moreover all say that manure is a very excellent thing in agriculture, and they also see it produced naturally; but nevertheless, though they know accurately how it is got, and though it is easy to make it abundant, some in this matter also take heed as to how it may be gathered, but others pay no heed. And yet the God above supplies rain, and all the hollow places become standing pools, and the land supplies vegetable matter of every sort, and he who intends to sow must cleanse the land; and, if a man were to cast into the water the matter which is cleared out of the way, time would itself forthwith produce that in which the ground delights For what kind of vegetable matter, or what kind of soil does not in standing water turn to manure? And all know too what an amount of attention the ground requires, as being too moist for sowing or too salt for planting in, and also how the water is drained off by trenches, and how the saltness is corrected by being mixed with all kinds of substances free from salt both moist and dry: but to these matters, too, some give heed and some do not. And if a man were altogether ignorant as to what the ground could produce, and had no opportunity of seeing any produce or plant from it, or of hearing the truth from anyone about it, would it not be much easier for any man to make trial of the ground than of a horse, and much easier than to make trial of a man? For there is nothing of which it makes a show with a view to deception, but in good faith it makes known clearly and truly what it can produce and what it cannot And the ground seems to me, too, to afford the best test of the bad and the good by making everything easy for them to discern and learn. For those who do not work have not, as in the case of the other arts, the excuse to make that they do not know how, and all are aware that ground well treated yields a good return, but laziness in agriculture is a clear indication of a worthless disposition. For no one tries to persuade himself of this, that a man could live without the necessaries of life; and it is clear that he who knows no other lucrative art, and who will not farm, intends to get his living by stealing or robbing or begging, or else is altogether unreasonable. And he added that it made a great difference as to agriculture being profitable or unprofitable whenever one man, having labourers more or less numerous, took some care that his workmen should be at their work during the regular time, and another man took no heed of this. For probably, while one man differs from ten others in working at the regular time, another man differs in going away before the time. And indeed, to allow the men to take things easily throughout the whole day, makes a difference of half in the whole work. Just as also, in travelling, sometimes men, who are both alike endowed in youth and health, in a distance of two hundred furlongs differ from each other in speed by a hundred furlongs, whenever the one by continually advancing is accomplishing the object for which he has started, and the other is listless in his disposition, and keeps resting both by fountains and in the shade and looks about him and courts gentle breezes. And so too in farming operations, those who do that at which they have been set to work, and those who do not do it, but find excuses for not working and for being allowed to take things easily, differ much in the matter of getting work finished. And then to work or to superintend well or badly involves indeed as great a difference as being wholly at work or wholly idle. For example, when men are digging in order that the vines may be clear of undergrowth, whenever they so dig that the undergrowth becomes more abundant and more luxuriant, how in that case could you help saying that the man was idle? These things are the causes of utter ruin to estates to a much greater extent than extreme ignorance For as to the fact that the outgoing expenses of the house continue undiminished, while the labour is not carried out profitably enough to balance the expense, one need no longer wonder if this produces a deficit instead of a surplus. My father, however, himself prosecuted that most effectual money-making which arises from farming to those who can be careful and farm earnestly, and also instructed me therein. For he never approved of my buying a well-tilled piece of land, but always urged me to buy any that, on account either of carelessness or of want of means on the part of the owners, was both untilled and unplanted. For he said that the well-tilled plots not only cost a great deal of money but admit of no improvement; and he considered that those which admit of no improvement do not afford the same pleasure either, but he deemed that all possessions and livestock that continue to improve are the source also of the greatest delight. Now nothing admits of more improvement than a piece of land which becomes entirely productive after lying untilled. For be well assured, Socrates, he continued, that I have ere this made many pieces of ground worth many times their original price. And this device, Socrates, he added, is of so great value, and so easy to learn too, that you now after hearing this will go away knowing it as well as I do, and will teach another, should you wish so to do. And my father also neither learnt this from another nor found it out by deep study; but he said that, from love of farming and of hard work, he desired a piece of ground of that sort, in order that he might at one and the same time have something to do and derive pleasure from making a profit. For in fact, Socrates, he added, my father was naturally, as it seems to me, fonder of farming than any other Athenian.

I, however, on hearing this, asked him: Whether was your father, Ischomachus, in the habit of retaining all the pieces of ground which he brought under cultivation, or used he to sell them too, if he obtained a good price?

He used assuredly to sell them too, said Ischomachus, but then he used at once to buy another instead, but one untilled, on account of his liking for work.

You tell me, Ischomachus, I said, that your father in reality naturally took no less interest in farming than merchants do in the corn trade. Now merchants, through being so exceedingly anxious to obtain corn, sail in quest of it to any place where they hear it is most abundant, crossing either the Ægæan or the Euxine or the Sicilian sea; and then, after taking on board as much as they can, they convey it by sea, and that too after putting it into the vessel by which they themselves sail. And they do not sell it too cheap in any chance quarter at random, whenever they want money, but they convey it and deliver it to the inhabitants of any place where they hear that corn is most highly valued and where people think most of it. And your father's love of farming seems to have been somewhat of this description.

To this Ischomachus replied: You are joking, Socrates; but I think that those also who sell their houses when they finish building them, and then build others, are no less fond of building.

Now assuredly, Ischomachus, I said, I tell you on my oath that I verily believe you, that all men are naturally fond of those things from which they think they can derive profit.

XXI.

Well, I am thinking, Ischomachus, I said, how well you have advanced your whole argument in support of your proposition. For you laid it down that the art of agriculture was the easiest of all to learn, and I have now been completely convinced by you from all that you have said that this is so.

But on this point assuredly, Socrates, said Ischomachus, which you know is common to all transactions, agricultural, political, domestic, and military—namely fitness to rule—I quite agree with you that some men differ greatly from others in this respect. For instance, he continued, in a trireme, when they are out at sea and must by rowing accomplish voyages that occupy a day, some of the commanders can say and do things to incite the men's minds to toil willingly, and others are so dull that they finish the same voyage in more than twice the time. And the former, both officer and men, disembark in a perspiration and with mutual congratulations; but the latter arrive cool, hating their superior officer and hated by him. And among generals, he said, some differ in this respect from others; for some make their men unwilling either to work or to incur danger, and make them disdain to obey, and unwilling to do so in any matter in which there is no necessity for it, and cause them even to boast of opposing their officer, and these same generals do not make them sensitive of disgrace either, if anything disgraceful occurs But again, the generals who are divinely great and excellent and skilful cause these same men, often also enlisting others in addition, to be deterred by shame from doing anything disgraceful, and also to think that it is better to obey, and to take pleasure in obeying individually, and in working unitedly not without spirit, whenever there is need to work. But just as a certain love of work arises in some private soldiers, so too in the whole army under good commanders there arises both the love of work and the ambition to be seen by the commander while doing some noble deed. And in fact those commanders to whom their followers are thus disposed become powerful commanders—not assuredly those of them who have the most robust bodily health of all the soldiers, and use the javelin and the bow with the greatest skill, and who, having a horse of the best quality, are in the forefront of the battle as riders or targeteers of the highest excellence; but those who can impress upon their soldiers the necessity of following both through fire and through every danger. A man would indeed rightly call these high-minded, one of whom many follow with unanimity; and he whose will many hands were ready to obey would justly be said to advance with a strong arm; and he who can accomplish great things by strength of will rather than by strength of body is a truly great man. And so too in domestic affairs, if the superintendent be a bailiff and also if he be a foreman, those who can make men willing and energetic at their work and persevering, are in fact the men whose efforts result in success, and who make the surplus large. And when, Socrates, he continued, the master, who can most severely punish the bad workman and also most highly reward the zealous, appears to inspect the work, if the workmen make no noticeable effort, I should not feel any admiration for him; but if, when they catch sight of him, they are spurred on, and ardour inspires each of the workmen, and mutual rivalry, and ambition severally to excel, I should say that this man has something of a kingly character. And this is a very great matter, as it seems to me, in every pursuit in which things are done by human labour, and in agriculture as well. However, I assuredly do not say that it is possible for a man to learn this also by seeing it done, or by once hearing about it, but I maintain that he who intends to attain proficiency in this needs instruction, and must be of a good disposition too, and, what is in fact most important, must be a heaven-born genius. For I do not at all think that this faculty of obtaining willing obedience is entirely human, but it is divine; and it is evidently given to those who have been truly initiated in wisdom. But to exercise a despotism over men against their will, they grant, as it seems to me, to those whom they consider worthy to live after the fashion in which Tantalus is said to pass eternity in Hades, fearing a second death.

BOOKS

FOR

London University Examinations

1888–89.

Published at

The University Correspondence College Office,

Cambridge.

University Correspondence College

TUTORIAL SERIES.

"The grand maxim of learning is to fix the mind on the right things To put it in a paradoxical form, to know what to forget is the secret of learning well"—REV. E. THRING.

The *Schoolmaster*, of May 21st, 1887, says.—"This series of Guides to the Examinations of London University will prove extremely serviceable to candidates. They are—as Guides should be—confessedly limited in scope, but they give just the kind of direction and advice that a student needs, pointing out the most reliable, helpful, and recent sources of information, and plainly indicating points of special importance In the Mathematical Guides for Matriculation and the Intermediate, the syllabus is divided up into weekly or fortnightly portions, and all the handbooks give sets of examination questions, with solutions to the exercises in mathematics. Drawn up in a useful and workmanlike fashion, the books give abundant proof of sound scholarship specialised and applied to the requirements of the London examinations. Speaking from the recollection of our own undergraduate days, it is painfully evident that such works as these would have saved us many an hour's hard and profitless grind. We can unreservedly commend the series, believing that such aids, supplemented by judicious teaching in weak subjects, may place a London degree within reach of a considerable number of our readers."

The *Educational Journal*, of the same date, says:—"These books save the student an immense labour, and, being from the pens of professional scholars, the information is not only correctly stated, but easily understood."

"I have looked through your Guides to London University Examinations, and I think them exceedingly good. The advice given is just of the right kind, and cannot fail to be useful. I shall have pleasure in recommending these little books."—H. S. HALL, M.A., Joint Author of Hall and Knight's Algebras and Hall and Stevens' Euclid.

University Correspondence College

TUTORIAL SERIES.

MATRICULATION MATHEMATICS.

On the same plan as Intermediate Mathematics, containing all the Questions from the last twenty Papers, and Solutions to Jan., 1887.

"Undoubtedly the candidate for Matriculation will find it good practice and training to work at a careful selection of old Matriculation Papers, and these, with much and judicious care, the editors of this book have selected. But they have done much more than this They give excellent advice as to the text-books to use, and then they lay out the students' work in the shape of 'Weekly Schemes of Study,' with the proper allowance of Matriculation Examination questions at every stage. The little book is an excellent daily companion for the candidate in his preparation."—*School Board Chronicle.*

B.A. MATHEMATICS, QUESTIONS AND SOLUTIONS.

Containing *all* the Papers in Pure Mathematics given at the B A Examinations, including 1886, with complete Solutions; and an article on Suitable Books for Private Students. Price 2s.

"The solutions are admirable, and cannot fail to be suggestive even to experienced mathematicians."—*Irish Teachers' Journal.*

"We can recommend this little volume to all whom it may concern." —*Practical Teacher.*

"This is an excellent little book, and, judiciously used, would be invaluable as a self-educator. There is nothing that so vividly brings before the student the nature of the ordeal which he has to undergo, as miscellaneous papers actually set in the School where he proposes to compete in mental gymnastics." — JOHN FINLAISON, M.A. Cantab. (late Examiner).

BOOKS FOR B.A.

B.A. Guides. Published the week following each Examination. CONTENTS: The Papers set at the Examination—Complete Solutions to the Mathematics—A Practical Guide to suitable books for private students preparing for the Examination, and of Authors prescribed for the next year. Price 2s. No. 1, October, 1887.

B.A. Mathematics, Questions and Solutions, Pure, from 1881 to 1886. Price 2s.

Mathematical Solutions for B.A. 1887, both Pure and Mixed, with article on Suitable Books. 2s.

B.A. Unseens. Being all the passages set from unprescribed Authors since first given. 2s.

Greek Examination Papers set at B.A. from 1874—1888, excluding Authors. 2s. (Ready in June.)

FOR B.A., 1888.

Sophocles.—Electra. An English Translation. Price 2s.

Demosthenes.—Androtion. An English Translation. Price 2s.

B.A. English. 1888. A Literal Translation of the more difficult parts of Alfred's "Orosius." By J. LOCKEY, M.A. (London). 1s.

Glossaries to Alfred's Orosius. 1s.

FOR 1889.

Aeschylus.—Agamemnon. A Translation. 2s.

Xenophon.—Oeconomicus. A Translation. 3s.

Juvenal.—The Satires. Set for 1889. A Translation. 2s.

B.A. English. Literal Renderings to the more difficult subjects set for 1889.

B.A. English Examination Questions (300) on the English subjects set for 1889. 2s. In preparation.

Synopsis of the Special Period of Greek History set for 1889. 1s.

Synopsis of the Special Period of Roman History set for 1889. 1s.

Test Papers on the Authors and Special Period in Greek and Latin. Ready July, 1888. 2s.

[illegible] application to

[illegible]

CPSIA information can be obtained at www.ICGtesting.com
Printed in the USA
LVOW022014080112

262908LV00014B/183/P

9 781176 897649